Hero Dogs

Hero Dogs

100 True Stories of Daring Deeds

Peter C. Jones and Lisa MacDonald

A High Tide Press Book
Andrews and McMeel
A Universal Press Syndicate Company
Kansas City

Photography Credits: Kathleen Campbell/Liaison 38-39TL; Mauro Carraro/Liaison 48; Linda Cataffo/Daily News 56, 57; Thomas J. Croke/Liaison 110-111; Anastasie Croy 68-69; Marcia Curtis/AP 72; Kyle Danaceau/AP 134; John Duricka/AP 140; John David Fleck/Liaison 26-27; Patrice Flesch 49, 98, 119, 137, 168; Harry Heleotis 138; Charles Kennedy/Liaison 66 (inset); Michael Kitada/The Orange County Register 20-21; Wernher Krutein/Liaison 54-55; Laguna Photo/Liaison 38-39B, 53T, 67B, 126-127, 142BL; Ron Levy/Liaison 67T; Brad Markel/Liaison 17; Cynthia Matthews 156; Peter D. Meltzer 176; Andrea Mohin 12-13, 14, 18-19, 22, 70; Chris Moorhead/Potomac News 88; Arthur Pollock/Boston Herald 42; Herbert George Ponting 24T, 128; Sheldon Secunda/Liaison 96-97; Art Seitz/Liaison 36; Dean Shalhoup/Liaison 73; Dale Spartas/Liaison 2, 8-9, 39TR, 53B, 95 (all), 174; Beth S. St. George 157; Mike Stephens/PA 16; Toni Tucker 6, 38BL, 52, 53 (inset), 81, 108, 109, 125, 142BR, 144-145; Chip Vinai/Liaison 94L; Ruby Washington/The New York Times 12 (inset); Zefiro & Luna/Liaison 80; AP 139; Corbis-Bettmann 40-41; Ken-L Ration 28, 32, 35, 44, 45, 58, 61, 62, 63, 64, 74, 76, 84, 86, 89, 92, 103, 104, 107, 112, 115, 118, 120, 121, 122, 130, 146, 151, 154, 162, 163, 165, 166, 169, 170; Guiding Eyes For The Blind 90; National Air And Space Museum 25, 82-83, 142T; National Archives 172 (all); Tass 160; The New York Times 158-159; Underwood & Underwood/Corbis-Bettman 24B; UPI/Corbis-Bettmann 79, 143; Courtesy: Larry Cohen 77, Captain Haggerty 164, New Jersey Newsphotos 37, Robert Schnelle 10-11, Cheryl Spardo 91, Emma Sweeney 152, Gail T. Tanis 150. All other photographs are courtesy of the dogs and their masters.

Designed by Doris Straus

ATTENTION: SCHOOLS AND BUSINESSES

Andrews and McMeel books are available at quantity discounts with bulk purchase for educational, business, or sales promotional use. For information write to:
Special Sales Department, Andrews and McMeel, 4520 Main Street,
Kansas City, Missouri 64111.

Library of Congress Cataloging-in-Publication Data
Jones, Peter C., Hero dogs : 100 true stories of daring deeds / Peter C. Jones and Lisa MacDonald.
p.   cm.
ISBN 0-8362-2720-4 (pbk.)
1. Dogs--Anecdotes. 2. Animal heroes--Anecdotes. I. MacDonald, Lisa. II. Title
SF426.J65 1997
636.7--dc20   96-43432
CIP

For Emma, Moxie and Rascal

Toni Tucker

TABLE OF CONTENTS

CHAPTER 1

The Professionals

Courtesy Robert Schnelle

A Hero for Our Times

New York, New York—Zeus is a member of the elite NYPD K-9 unit. The four-year-old German shepherd is a peerless tracker who can locate evidence of any sort in any setting. With a nose like a one-dog crime scene laboratory, Zeus can identify a suspect who has dropped a hat or gun and then pursue, corner and detain the fugitive until his partner, Robert Schnelle, reaches the scene.

Working on a tip from an informant, the canine sleuth located the body of Nelson Figueroa, who had been missing for eight years. Zeus found the victim in a four-foot grave, stuffed in a plastic bag with his skull crushed by a baseball bat. After Zeus located the body, the murderer was extradited from Florida.

With the rise of terrorist attacks, Zeus's job description has expanded to include search and rescue. He participated in the rescue effort and later the investigation of the World Trade Center bombing. An indispensable member of the Federal Emergency Management Agency (FEMA), Zeus was sent to Oklahoma City in the aftermath of the 1995 bombing. Searching the rubble for survivors, he located twenty-four bodies.

Schnelle bought Zeus as a puppy so that he could train him from scratch. After three months Zeus could find and track. He joined the department shortly after his first birthday and continues to live with the Schnelles. Their two children think he is a swell pal as well as a great cop.

Andrea Mohin

Andrea Mohin

Stop, Drop and Roll

Brooklyn, New York—Hooper, a six-year-old Dalmatian and a second-generation fire dog, has lived at Engine Company 211 since he was a pup. Hooper is an educator. He works the elementary school circuit with his handler Ken Hanifin teaching lifesaving techniques.

Recently, Hooper visited a school in Staten Island after the kids had seen an elderly man emerge on fire from his house across the street. The man later died and the children were traumatized. Hooper alleviated their fears by teaching them to stop, drop and roll, which demonstrated how they could survive a fire.

Since appearing on David Letterman's show, Hooper has become a celebrity, but he is still content to hang with his pals in Williamsburg, Brooklyn.

Winner of the 1995 Isaac Liberman Civil Service Award

Lab Blasts Bombers

Mike Stephens/PA

Londonberry, Northern Ireland—Jason, a bomb-sniffing Labrador retriever, discovered a 150-pound bomb in a dustbin literally seconds before terrorists detonated it by remote control. The dog wagged his tail in warning, saving the lives of five nearby soldiers who dove for cover to escape the blast, which was heard twenty miles away. The heroic seven-year-old canine soldier was tossed high into the air but miraculously survived with only a concussion. His handler, Lance Corporal Simon Doyle, who was one of the fortunate five, said, "His job means our lives, but to him it's just a big game and he loves it." An army spokesman hailed the dog a hero: "The soldiers would almost certainly have died, or been seriously injured, but for Jason."
Winner 1989 Pro Dog Devotion to Duty Medal

The Fastest Nose in the West

South Texas—After he sniffed out $128 million in Mexican cocaine in eleven months, cranky drug dealers put out a $30,000 contract on Rocky, a Belgian Malinois. Undeterred, the best narc in South Texas just keeps on sniffing.

Brad Markel/Liaison

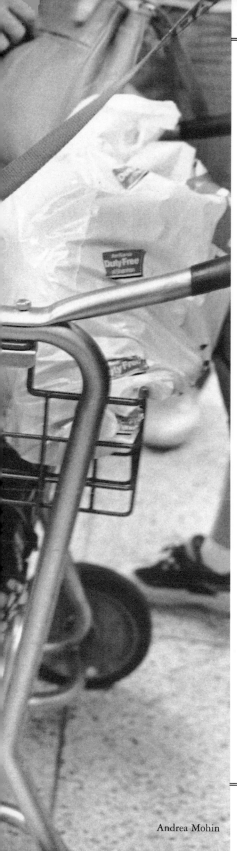
Andrea Mohin

Caps Puts Cap on Contraband

Queens, New York—Standing only two feet tall, Caps, an astonishingly cute beagle, cleared more than 320,000 passengers on 1,650 flights while making 3,500 busts during his first eleven months on the case at Kennedy Airport. A rising star in the USDA K-9 Beagle Brigade, Caps sniffs baggage for illegally imported food, plants and birds.

With his finely tuned investigative tool, Caps can detect the scent of an apple removed from luggage three days before. When Caps finds contraband, he sits down and looks up at his handler, Martin Queller, who then inspects the baggage.

Beagles were selected for this sensitive mission because they do not intimidate passengers in crowded airports. Even an eleven-year-old boy caught with a forbidden apple was unable to hold a grudge. Says his human partner, "Caps is so cute, people don't mind getting busted by him."

Michael Kitada/The Orange County Register

The $85 Million Nose

Orange County, California—Sometimes it takes a while to find the right career. Winston, a pedigreed yellow Labrador, failed as a show dog, hunting dog and family pet. Ultimately, he found his calling as a crackerjack drug buster, so hated by drug traffickers that a $50,000 bounty was placed on his head.

In his extraordinary career Winston sniffed out $44 million of illegal drugs plus a nearly equal amount of confiscated cash and property, bringing his total haul to over $85 million. Together with his partner, Don Lambert, the brilliant dog took part in the prosecution of thirteen hundred criminals. A judge once said, "Winston has more credibility than most of the witnesses who have appeared before me."

Drug dealers desperately tried to foil the canine enforcer by shrouding their stashes with pepper, mothballs, garlic, coffee and even Vicks Vaporub. But Winston couldn't be fooled. Incredibly, he was even able to identify the scent of illegal drugs on money that had passed through the hands of drug traffickers.

Winston undertook yet one more career, as a heroic role model to children. Visiting with his partner, he demonstrated his olfactory prowess, encouraging children to join him in the war against drugs.

Andrea Mohin

An Arsonist's Worst Nightmare

Brooklyn, New York—When a fire seems suspicious, Fire Marshall Fred, a four-year-old black Labrador, gets a call. After his handler releases him at the scene, Fred begins his arson investigation, sniffing for accelerants such as gasoline. If Fred sits down, he has determined the fire's point of origin and the presence of an accelerant. Later Fred may be asked to sniff out a suspect in a lineup. "I train him every day," says his handler. "When he leads us to an arsonist, all that training becomes worthwhile."

Herbert George Ponting

Vida, Captain Smith's top dog during the 1910-1913 South Polar Expedition.

Los Angeles, California—Battling Von, a ten-month-old German shepherd, slugged it out with Ralph Miller for four rounds at the 1926 West Coast Juvenile Police Dog Welterweight Championship. The boxers fought to a draw.

Booster, regular canine copilot for Charles Lindbergh, joins "The Lone Eagle" for preflight conference in Bird City, Kansas, circa 1922.

CHAPTER 2

Devotion

Zorro Stops Spin Cycle

Orangevale, California— Mark Cooper owes his life to Zorro, his German shepherd/ wolf mix. After falling eighty-five feet into a ravine, he landed, unconscious, in a dangerous whirlpool. Zorro dove in and pulled him out of the swirling water. While Cooper's hiking companion went for help, the loyal dog slept on top of the injured man to keep him warm. When the rescue vehicle arrived, there was no room for Zorro. Later, when two volunteers from the Sierra Club went back for the dog, they found the faithful Zorro guarding his master's abandoned backpack.

1976 Ken-L Ration Dog Hero of the Year Runner-up

The Incredible Journey

Silverton, Oregon—Loyalty knows no bounds. When Bobbie, a Scottish collie mix, was separated from his family on a trip to Indiana, he spent the next six months traveling three thousand miles cross country to return home.

Witnesses who helped recreate the journey determined that the faithful dog had battled the rapids of the White River, crossed the Mississippi and the Rockies and even walked out on a family that wanted to adopt him. Increasingly weary, with the pads of his paws worn to the bone, Bobbie accepted help for his injuries in Portland, then took to the road for the final leg of his journey to Silverton.

To the astonishment of his family, he returned home. The exhausted dog lived long enough to enjoy his homecoming, but the journey had taken its toll. Bobbie died at the tender age of six with the full and complete knowledge that "there's no place like home." A simple memorial in Portland honors this devoted dog whose fame spread across the nation back in 1923 and whose legend lives on.

Legendary Loyalty

Tokyo, Japan—Although Hachi-ko has been dead for more than thirty years, memories of his heroic loyalty continue to capture the Japanese imagination. He lives today on stage and screen, in literature and song, and in the hearts of millions of children.

Each morning, Hachi-ko, a golden-brown Akita, would accompany his beloved master, Tokyo University professor Eisaburo Ueno, to the train and in the afternoon return to Shibuya Station to meet the professor and walk home. All who witnessed this daily ritual marveled at the dog's devotion.

Sadly, one lovely May day in 1925, the professor died unexpectedly in his laboratory. Hachi-ko came to meet the train that afternoon and every morning and afternoon for the next ten years. Word spread throughout the world. A statue honoring "Faithful Dog Hachi-ko" was commissioned by the Los Angeles Friends of Animals and erected at Shibuya Station.

A year later, Hachi-ko missed his first train. The ailing dog was found lying in a nearby lane, but died later that day. Today Hachi-ko and his legend are everywhere. Recently, an old recording of Hachi-ko's bark was discovered, repaired with laser surgery, and broadcast to the nation, for whom the spirit of Hachi-ko's undying loyalty continues to set a powerful example.

Mother's Little Helper

New York, New York—On the good mornings at the Held house, six-year-old Brendan would wake with the sun and shriek, "It's daytime!!" The bad mornings were another story. Brendan would growl like a bear while his mother tried to coax him into his socks in time for the school bus. Inevitably, the bus was missed, the morning was a catastrophe and everyone was weary before the day had begun.

Meanwhile, the Helds made the best decision of their family life. They bought a dog. Emma's arrival brought an unexpected bonus: the feisty border terrier volunteered for the dangerous mission of awakening their unpredictable son. And Brendan liked it!

Each morning the little dog waits patiently for her cue from the boy's mother: "Emma, go wake Brendan." Now the Helds rest easy with happy noises coming from their son's room. And they get to sleep for another forty-nine seconds.

The Dog Who Refused to Quit

Spanaway, Washington—Patches, a collie/malamute mix, showed super canine strength and perseverance in an amazing series of rescues that saved his drowning master, Marvin Scott. One cold December night with the thermometer hovering around zero, Patches tagged along as Scott walked down to the pier below their lakeside home to check on possible ice damage to a patrol boat.

Spray from the lake had made the pier dangerously slick, and ice was forming around the boat. As Scott pulled on the stern line to free his boat, he slipped and pitched forward onto the floating dock below, ripping tendons and muscles in both of his legs. Momentum from the fall caused him to roll off the floating dock and sink into the frigid water.

Miraculously, Scott felt someone grasp him by his hair. It was Patches. Navigating the icy water, the dog pulled his dazed and shivering master to the surface and then towed him to the edge of the floating dock. Dimly aware that the wearied dog was nearly drowning, Scott managed to push Patches up onto the dock.

But Scott's legs were useless. Attempting to pull himself onto the dock, he blacked out and fell back into the deadly lake. The fearless dog dove in instantly, again seized him by the hair, and towed him back to the dock. The exhausted man helped his dog back onto the dock and then hung on grimly, screaming for help. But with the wind against him, his cries went unheard.

Bracing his feet firmly on the dock, Patches grasped Scott's collar and tugged with all his strength, encouraging the struggling Scott to make one more try. Somehow, between the two of them, the gasping man was able to haul his body out of the water.

With Patches tenaciously gripping his master's collar, Scott began crawling on his elbows up the rock-studded three-hundred-foot slope toward his house. Finally, the agonized man was close enough to throw a stone against the back door and alert his wife.

Scott hovered between life and death for twenty-five days. Massive operations were required on both of his legs. Seven months later, walking with two canes, he was able to return to work.

1965 Ken-L Ration Dog Hero of the Year

Fritzie's Honor

Queens, New York—Herman died in the early fall. He had not been feeling well for some time, but his death came as a shock. Ilse, his wife of forty years, left with no one to share the events of the day, was devastated. She wore a brave face for her daughter Doris, but clearly she felt the best days of her life had ended.

Her daughter made repeated attempts to lift Ilse's spirits, but nothing worked. One day, Doris asked, "Would you like a dog?" The next week, her mother quietly said, "Maybe I would like a little dog."

Doris found Fritzie at the Humane Society. He had been abandoned in the park and, although loved by all at the shelter, the King Charles spaniel mix had been awaiting a new home for six weeks.

For a young dog, Fritzie had encountered more than his share of trouble and was terrified on the ride home. Fritzie and Ilse met in the yard. They stopped and looked into each other's eyes. Somehow they knew. Meaning has returned to Ilse's life and the once-terrified little dog finally has a real home.

Beggar Bites Bobby

Carmichael, California—Beggar, a 165-pound St. Bernard owned by Mr. and Mrs. Robert Mitchell, saved their son, Bobby, from a watery death. While his mother was busy with housework, the three-year-old wandered away from home and became hopelessly lost. A search party failed to find any trace of the boy.

Finally, a Boy Scout troop, encamped along the rain-swollen American River, came across Bobby and Beggar, both soaking wet, more than a mile from home. Leading the shivering tot by his sleeve, with her protective instincts fully aroused, the massive dog refused to surrender her little charge to the unfamiliar Scouts. However, once Beggar recognized a family friend, the dog docilely released Bobby and trotted home after them.

When his parents stripped off Bobby's wet clothing, teeth marks on his body confirmed the young boy's story of how he had fallen into the river and how Beggar, seizing him in her huge jaws, had swum him to safety.

1962 Ken-L Ration Dog Hero of the Year

Mother of the Year

Art Seitz/Liaison

Oakland Park, Florida—Tethered to her leash, Sheba, a Rottweiler mix, was forced to watch as her owner buried her nine squealing puppies in a sandy, backyard grave. Somehow, the frantic first-time mother broke free and furiously dug through the dirt to find her litter alive in a large paper sack.

"It was a mother's determination," said veterinarian Cindy Bossart, who monitored the puppies at the Animal Hospital in Fort Lauderdale. "In seventeen years of practice, I've never come across anything like this before." The paper sack apparently held an air pocket, and seasonably cool temperatures probably helped to slow the puppies' metabolism.

"I know dogs," reflected a puzzled Bossart, "they love unconditionally. Too bad we're not more like them."

Police removed Sheba, her puppies and a Doberman pinscher from the home of the owner. The Broward Sheriff's Office Animal Abuse Unit was flooded with calls from people anxious to adopt the dogs.

A Loyal Brother

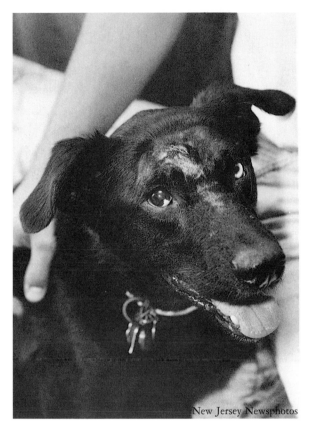

New Jersey Newsphotos

Newark, New Jersey—It's a good thing that Blackball wasn't blackballed from the Pi Kappa Phi fraternity house at the New Jersey Institute of Technology after a fraternity brother rescued him half-starved from the street. Although Blackball has never quite managed to graduate, he is the frat's most senior resident and its most loyal.

When fraternity brothers Bassem Hanna and Paul Santos were accosted by a gun-wielding thief, Blackball, a Labrador/husky mix, stormed out the front door to intervene. The startled gunman fired and missed, then fired again, turned and fled. Blackball took the second round in the head, staggered forward and fell to the ground.

Minutes later, Brother Blackball struggled to his feet. Surgery repaired the entrance and exit wounds the near-lethal bullet had made in his face. Regrettably, the thug was never apprehended.

Kathleen Campbell

Toni Tucker

Dale Spartas/Liaison

Dale Spartas (T) and Laguna Photo (B)/Liaison

Sixth Sense

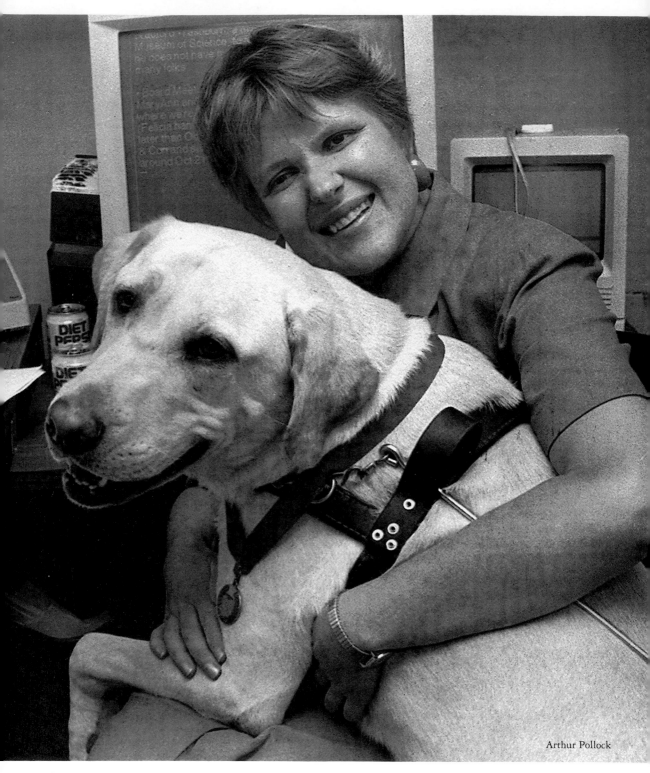

Arthur Pollock

Shadow Senses Danger in Darkness

Boston, Massachusetts—Legally blind Emily Larson was saved from a murderous stalker by the protective instincts of her Seeing Eye dog, a yellow Lab named Shadow.

For years she had been plagued by a former client's unwanted attention. Abruptly, the man's obsession became ominous. Emily alerted the police, who could do little until the stalker acted.

Before dawn Emily got up as usual, but Shadow refused to go out, blocked the open door and began barking furiously. Emily called the police: "My dog is going wild. I think he's found the stalker."

An officer found the man lurking across the street with knives and hammers concealed under his coat. He later confessed and was convicted of attempted murder.

1992 Massachusetts SPCA Gold Medal

Keg Saves Karen in Kelly Creek

Bozeman, Montana—While her mother was out shopping, eighteen-month-old Karen McMannis was left in the care of her neighbor. Playing with her inseparable German shepherd companion, Keg, the girl roamed out the backyard onto a footbridge that spanned Kelly Creek. The normally sedate stream was roaring at flood stage. As she toddled along the bridge, the tot lost her balance and fell backward into the torrent.

Dumbstruck with fear, the neighbor saw the immense dog leap into the angry waters after the child. Reaching her side, Keg attempted to seize her dress, but could not manage a secure grip. Instead, he clamped his teeth into her shoulder blade and with powerful strokes, begin swimming steadily toward the shore as they were swept downstream. Battling the current with furious determination, he towed the unconscious child to shore and pulled her partway onto the riverbank so that the neighbor could reach them. Four hours later, a Bozeman hospital pronounced Karen out of danger.

1960 Ken-L Ration Dog Hero of the Year

The Protector of Children

Denison, Texas—Tang, a huge, friendly collie, adopted by Air Force Captain and Mrs. Maurice Dyer, had an uncanny ability to sense when a child was in danger, saving no fewer than five youngsters from severe injury or death.

Before his adoption Tang had been abused and was completely mistrustful of humans, especially children. However, "something in his eyes" reminded the Dyers of their own lost dog, and with numerous misgivings, they took him home.

Affection and tender care worked wonders on Tang. Within six months he had developed into a powerful but friendly dog. Without any prompting from the Dyers, Tang commissioned himself the "Protector of Children" at the airbase.

Once, barking loudly, Tang planted himself squarely in front of a milk truck and refused to budge. When the puzzled driver went to investigate, he found that a two-year-old girl had climbed onto the back of his truck and would almost certainly have fallen. When she was removed, Tang ceased his barking and lay placidly on the sidewalk.

When the news came that Tang had been unanimously selected as the first winner of the Ken-L Ration Dog Hero Award, the neighborhood children organized an impromptu parade in his honor.

1954 Ken-L Ration Dog Hero of the Year

Soothsayer Rottie Saves Fallen Fireman

Cucamonga, California—About half an hour into a three-hour hike with his four-year-old Rottweiler, Cinder, fireman Lorenzo Abundiz noticed that the big dog seemed sick and decided to turn around. Ironically, it was Cinder's way of telling his master to go home. A few minutes after returning to the house, Abundiz collapsed with a heart attack and lost consciousness. He awoke to find Cinder nudging the phone toward him and managed to dial 911 for help. "I strongly believe dogs can sense when your body chemistry is going haywire," said the grateful Abundiz, "Cinder saved my life." Cinder had been a gift from fellow firefighter Mark Eide. Abundiz had pulled Eide from a burning building after part of it collapsed on top of him.

1994 Ken-L Ration Dog Hero of the Year Runner-up

Sibling Savant

Saginaw, Michigan—Buffy, a terrier mix, demonstrated that a dog can be a dog's best friend when he saved his canine sibling, Corky. When their owner, Dawn Ramey, opened the front door to call the dogs, Corky was nowhere to be found. Buffy suddenly began pulling on Dawn's pant leg, urging her to follow. She led Dawn to the sidewalk where a snowbank had just been created by a city plow. The little dog began digging furiously, finally uncovering a frightened and chilled-to-the-bone Corky. The grateful Dawn rushed the reunited twosome into the warmth of their home.

1982 Ken-L Ration Dog Hero of the Year Runner-up

Silence Is Golden

New Orleans, Louisiana—This thug got what he deserved after forcing Dr. Chris Eschenberg to unlock his apartment door. Eschenberg's three-year-old Chesapeake Bay retriever, Oskar, typically barks and playfully fusses when he hears his master's key in the lock. This night he was silent. As the robber stepped into the apartment, the dog lunged and grabbed the man's forearm with his teeth. The would-be thief somehow managed to break free and fled.

1995 Ken-L Ration Dog Hero of the Year Runner-up

Irish Lass Foils Arsonist

Garden City, South Carolina—Mixed breed Rosie O'Grady alerted her owner Cheryl Essex to the threat of arsonists by frantically running back and forth on the porch of their third-floor apartment while barking wildly in a strange high pitch. Essex immediately called the police, who found that arsonists had packed the building's stairwells with gasoline-saturated towels and had poured gasoline around the cars in the parking lot as well. The arsonists fled, literally one match from catastrophe. Rosie's quick work saved thirty-six condominiums and many lives.

1993 Ken-L Ration Dog Hero of the Year Runner-up

That's Some Buddy!

Raleigh, North Carolina—When Buddy returned home, he immediately sensed that his owner was in grave danger. The 108-pound Bernese mountain dog crashed through a glass storm door and ran to the bedroom to find his mistress, Peggy Satterwhite, beaten, bound and gagged. Knowing Buddy meant business, the menacing intruder fled through the bedroom window.

1989 Ken-L Ration Dog Hero of the Year Runner-up

Baby's Early Warning

Mauro Carraro/Liais

London, England—Bonnie Whitfield could not understand why her dog Baby kept sniffing at a mole on her thigh. But Baby's persistent interest in Bonnie's little mole led her husband John to take her to the hospital. Dr. Andres Pembrocke suspected that the mole might be malignant and decided to remove it. Tests showed that Dr. Pembrocke's suspicions were accurate and the early removal saved Bonnie's life.

Calling All Canines

Patrice Flesch

Morey's Pond, Massachusetts—At two in the morning Kid Charlemagne, a.k.a. K.C., uncharacteristically awoke from a sound sleep and began barking at his master, Roland Cloutier. Although the man tried to get back to sleep, the Dalmatian took matters into his own teeth and dragged Cloutier by the pajama sleeve over to the bedroom window overlooking the pond.

In the early morning gloom the man could just make out the desperate struggle taking place in the frigid water below. Cloutier ran out of the house and heard the distant cries of a panicked dog unable to find his way to shore. He summoned police, who rescued the stray and took him to a veterinarian. Chubs, the rescued black Labrador, is alive and well because K.C. sensed a fellow canine in distress.

1993 Massachusetts SPCA Gold Medal

Eastsiders Saved by Bomb-Sniffing Airedale

New York, New York—Eastsiders Nancy and Bill Evans have always walked their eight-year-old Airedale—a girl named George after a great line of lady Georges: George Sand, George Eliot, and Nancy's outrageous Aunt Gigi—in front of St. Ignatius Loyola Church on Park Avenue. However, last Saturday night George inexplicably hit the brakes and refused to go anywhere near the church.

After a circuitous walk, the puzzled couple went to bed. As they were dozing off, an enormous explosion rattled the windows, filling the air with smoke. They got dressed, put a leash on George, and went out to investigate. George led them to the church where a Plymouth Duster, demolished by a car bomb, lay smoldering in front of the now-blackened steps. No one was hurt, but the bombers escaped and remain at large.

George enjoyed elevated status at home and was rewarded with a bone from the butcher.

Toni Tucker (left & inset)

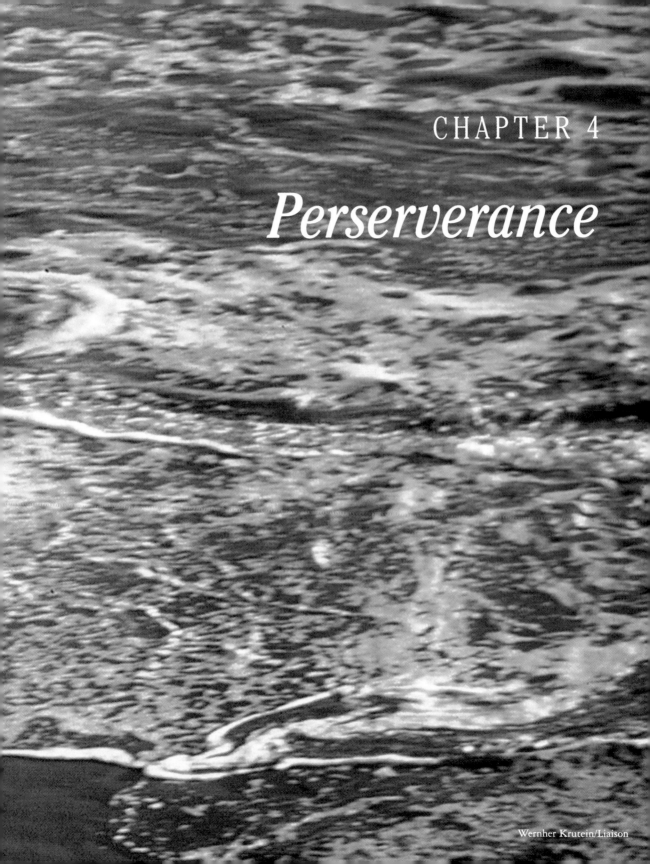

CHAPTER 4

Perserverance

Wernher Krutein/Liaison

Linda Cataffo

The Dynamic Duo

New York, New York—Who says New Yorkers are afraid to get involved? When Buzz, a 140-pound bull mastiff, and his five-foot, two-inch mistress, Mary Ann Dennis, observed a mugging in the park the dynamic duo didn't think twice and set off in hot pursuit. When the thief jumped into a taxi, Dennis convinced the driver of a van to join in the chase. The van finally overtook the taxi, but the cabby said that the bandit had already fled. Losing hope, Buzz and Dennis continued their chase on foot. Spotting the robber climbing into another cab, Buzz leapt in front of the taxi as Dennis yelled, "Stop, that man robbed somebody!" The suspect stuck his head out the window and began to threaten both girl and beast. The intrepid pair stood their ground. Fortuitously, police arrived and handcuffed the thief.

Ride 'Em Kenny

Livingston, Montana—Chester, a Chesapeake Bay retriever, retrieved five-year-old Kenny Homme from a swollen creek near his house. His mother, who had been washing dishes and periodically glancing out the window to check on her son, suddenly noticed that he was gone. Running outside, she heard his cries, "Help me! Save me!"

The boy had slid down a steep hill, fallen into the surging creek below, and was struggling to stay afloat. Fortunately, Chester had run after him and made a flying leap into the turbulent water. As the dog swam toward Kenny, the powerful current pulled the boy into a culvert. Kenny twice grabbed his dog's hair, only to lose his grip. After ten minutes, the exhausted child was finally able to climb onto the dog's back and literally rode him out of the tunnel to safety. "If we didn't have Chester," said Mrs. Homme, "we wouldn't have a son."

1978 Ken-L Ration Dog Hero of the Year

All About Eve

Indianapolis, Indiana—As they set off on an all-night drive to an antique show, Kathie Vaughn and Eve, her 104-pound Rottweiler, could never have imagined that they were in for the nightmare of their lives.

Twenty minutes down the road, Vaughn, who is paralyzed from the waist down, heard an explosion and her specially equipped truck veered out of control. Somehow she managed to stop the vehicle, threw open the passenger door and ordered her dog out of the smoke-filled cabin. Alone in the truck, Vaughn frantically struggled to reassemble her wheelchair.

Sensing imminent danger, Eve dove back into the car and grabbed her mistress's arm. Fearing for the dog's safety, Vaughn screamed, "No!" But Eve wouldn't stop. Ultimately, the dog seized Vaughn by her paralyzed leg, hauled her from the truck, and, as the woman blacked out, pulled her ten feet away. Vaughn came to just in time to witness a massive explosion. Frightened by their proximity to the blast and the fifty-foot flames shooting out of the truck, Eve dragged the paralyzed woman a further twenty feet.

The dog was so protective toward her owner that she menaced the arriving police and at first refused to let them carry her injured mistress to the squad car. "They say dogs have no reasoning power," said a grateful Kathie Vaughn, "but I pushed her out of the truck and she returned, against all her natural instincts, to save me."

1992 William O. Stillman Award

The Disobedient Duo

Dickenson, North Dakota—One cold, blustery December day in a sparsely populated section of North Dakota, Laura Schmidt's seven-year-old terrier, Champ, and his partner in crime Buddy, a three-year-old mutt, conspired to disobey their mistress in order to save a man's life.

When Laura went to call the dogs in, there was no response. Puzzled, she went out in search of the pair. Eventually, she found them barking and circling an isolated warehouse. When she called out again, they refused to come and ran to the door. Resigned, Laura gave up calling and started following.

The dogs led her into the building where she found injured freight driver Marvin Decar. The trucker had been trying to hoist a ninety-two-inch, 2,680-pound tire when the tire slipped and smashed his foot, pinning it against his thigh. Terrified he would not be found, he had managed to light a small fire in hope of attracting attention.

Laura ran for her husband and, together, they freed Marvin from beneath the tire and took him to a nearby hospital where he underwent surgery on his foot. The doctors said that Marvin would have gone into shock and died from loss of blood if Champ and Buddy hadn't been so heroically disobedient.

1986 Ken-L Ration Dog Hero of the Year

Buddy Saves Billies at Bud Lake

Bud Lake, New Jersey—Buddy is one dedicated farm dog. Early one morning barks from the twenty-month-old collie roused his masters, Mr. and Mrs. Matthew Crinkley, to a disaster in progress. The Crinkleys rushed to their bedroom window in time to see the walls and roof of their goat maternity barn collapse into a flaming pile of ruin.

Aghast, the terrified couple raced outside. There, with the efficiency of a Prussian general, was Buddy, marching back and forth, tending the entire flock of seventy expectant mother goats whom he had herded out of the barn. Despite suffering from smoke inhalation and severe burns to his paws, Buddy had maneuvered the herd of notoriously stubborn animals to safety.

However, sparks had begun to ignite the roof of the second barn that housed their remaining brood of thirty goats. Fortunately, this brave and devoted dog barked to warn the Crinkleys, giving them enough time to wet down the shingles to prevent the fire from spreading and ensure, come spring, that the flock would flourish.

1964 Ken-L Ration Dog Hero of the Year

The Littlest Firefighter

Danbury, Connecticut—Standing just twelve inches high at the shoulder, Mimi, an apricot-colored miniature poodle, sounded the alarm, saving eight people from a fiery death.

The poodle, purchased only four months earlier, frantically roused owner Nicholas Emerito, who had dozed off on the living room couch. He rushed to the first floor bedroom to alert his wife and young son, Peter, while Mimi, ignoring dense smoke and flames, dashed up the steep stairway. Racing from room to room, she awakened the three Emerito girls, Deborah, Lisa and Patricia, and their brothers, Edward and Anthony.

Accompanied by Mimi, Edward and the girls groped their way down the stairs, but inadvertently left Anthony behind. Sputtering and choking, Edward started back up the stairs, but Mimi dashed past him. As Edward reached the door to their bedroom, he saw Mimi frantically jumping up and down on the bed and barking to awaken his brother.

The boy, in his drowsy state, had assumed it was all a nightmare and had gone back to sleep. Finally fully awake, the two boys followed Mimi through the smoke until their escape route was suddenly cut off. The boys retreated to their bedroom, clambered out the window to the roof and leapt to safety while Mimi fled beneath the smoke. The reunited family watched silently as the fire consumed their home.

Ironically, until the night of the fire, Mimi had steadfastly refused to walk up or down the stairway, and had insisted on being carried. Yet, with flames and smoke filling the stairway the gallant little poodle traversed it four times to save the family she loved.

1972 Ken-L Ration Dog Hero of the Year

One Convincing Lady

Mehlville, Missouri—One dark, cold February afternoon, three-year-old Tommy Abel wandered away from his home, accompanied by his lovable mutt, Lady. Tommy's parents organized a search party that failed to find the pair.

The tot, who had found himself farther from home than anyone imagined, was mired in a swamp. Exhausted, the spent child could no longer even cry for help. Lady, who had been watching his unsuccessful efforts to free himself, hurried away. But this was no abandonment of her little master.

Racing through the desolate woods, Lady happened upon two telephone linemen. Barking and whining, the dog dashed back and forth signaling that she wished to be followed. Finally convinced, they shouldered their equipment and trudged after her.

Just before deciding that Lady was leading them on a wild goose chase, they reached the crest of a hill and there below them was Tommy, up to his knees in the sticky mud, unable to utter a sound. As darkness closed around them, they finally freed the boy and brought him home to his nearly frantic parents.

Winner 1959 Ken-L Ration Dog Hero of the Year

Ron Levy (T), Laguna Photo (B) & Charles Kennedy (inset)/Liaison

Anastasie Crov

CHAPTER 5

Sickness and Health

Andrea Mohin

Therapy Dog Feels Patients' Pain

Stamford, Connecticut—Perri, a therapy dog, has helped many nursing home patients to exorcise their pain and loneliness. The five-year-old champion bichon frise is often involved in group therapy sessions, moving from lap to lap as patients relive fond moments with their loved ones.

Following a traumatic fall, an elderly lady was comforted by Perri. The woman, who had previously had difficulty confronting her pain, held Perri as she cried and cried about how hard it is to be old, confined to a nursing home and lonely. A social worker observing the scene said, "Therapy dogs allow people to get in touch with their feelings."

Dog Calls 911

Dean Shalhoup/Nashua

Nashua, New Hampshire—"Engine Six, you may have to use forcible entry because a dog just called 911."

Yes, it's really true. Lyric, a golden-haired Irish setter, has risen to fame for summoning rescuers by autodialing 911 with her paw. Her mistress, Judi Bayly, suffers from both sleep apnea and asthma, a serious combination of conditions that can even stop her breathing. Consequently, the woman spends the night hooked up to an oxygen machine. When the machine failed, thereby sounding an alarm, Lyric did the job she was trained to do.

The devoted setter knocked the handset off the telephone and pawed the keys preset to dial 911. When the dispatcher answered, Lyric barked into the phone. This was not the first time that this miracle dog had sprung into action. Several weeks earlier, Lyric had summoned help when she found her mistress in full cardiac arrest.

Although the dog became a media star, she'd rather be home at night with her mistress than sitting next to Jay Leno on the Tonight Show. "She's like my little guardian angel. She's with me more than my husband, more than my kids, more than anyone else in my life."

However, Lyric's heroism does have one drawback. The telephone receiver has been regularly bitten, dropped on the floor and drowned in the water dish. Judy is on her third special telephone but says, "It's a small price to pay for my own live-in lifesaver."

Rottweiller Comforts Quaking Child

Watsonville, California—Reona, a two-and-a-half-year-old Rottweiller, showed intelligence and bravery during a devastating earthquake. Hearing screams from across the street after the earth's first jolt, Reona bolted out the door, jumped three fences and bounded into the home of five-year-old Vivian Cooper.

The terrified child, who suffers from potentially fatal epileptic seizures often triggered by excitement, was standing in the kitchen when the 102-pound Reona pushed her against the cabinets and sat on her. Seconds later, a large microwave oven on top of the refrigerator came crashing down just where Vivian had been standing.

Although Vivian had been afraid of Reona in the past, she hugged the dog tightly and buried her head into Reona's fur as the big dog calmed the frightened youngster. "Now there's a bond between them that just won't quit," said Jim Patton, Reona's proud owner.

1989 Ken-L Ration Dog Hero of the Year

The Terrible Tonsillectomy

San Carlos, California—Six-year-old Gary Gustafson survived a medical emergency thanks to his Shetland sheepdog Lassie, who showed good judgment by breaking a house rule in order to save her beloved master. She had been taught never to enter Mr. and Mrs. Gustafson's bedroom; instead, she would settle herself near Gary's door, not budging until morning.

Late one night, Gary's parents were roused from a deep slumber by Lassie, who had rushed into their bedroom, barking, whining and pulling at their pajamas. Astounded by the dog's strange actions, they ordered her to return to her post outside Gary's bedroom at the far end of the house. But Lassie stubbornly refused to leave and the intensity of her cries only increased.

They thought that she might need to go outside, but as Mr. Gustafson led her to the door, she began racing up and down the hall that led to Gary's bedroom. With a sigh of resignation, Mr. Gustafson followed her into his son's room, and was horrified to find the boy lying on the floor in a pool of blood, hemorrhaging from a recent tonsillectomy. Gary was rushed to the hospital where the terrified parents learned that a further fifteen-minute delay would have cost their son his life.

Gary had been offered his choice of the litter. The puppy that caught his fancy was small and rather sickly, but he loved her on sight and refused to consider the more healthy looking dogs. In the end Lassie proved to be the prize of the litter.

1956 Ken-L Ration Dog Hero of the Year

The Blood Donor

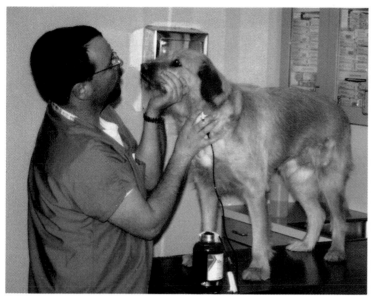

Larchmont, New York—Willie, a six-year-old Airedale mix, has a day job. Every morning this professionally fulfilled terrier accompanies his master, veterinarian Larry Cohen, to the animal hospital, where he is available to give transfusions to needy dogs. Most recently, Willie donated blood to Sebastian, who was bleeding to death from a tumor in the stomach. Thanks to Willie, the dog was diagnosed and rushed into surgery in time to save his life. "Willie is always willing to come to work with me even though he never knows from day to day if he will be poked and prodded," says Dr. Cohen. "He seems to understand that this is just part of his role in life."

Willie, abandoned on the streets of Phoenix, Arizona, was rescued by the Animal Benefits Club, who brought him to Dr. Cohen for treatment. He was not only cured from the often-fatal parvovirus, but found a home as well. "I had treated hundreds of animals for the ABC over the years, but Willie really caught my eye," remembers Dr. Cohen. "I decided it was time to add a puppy to our menagerie of four cats and a young son, so I applied to adopt him. ABC required that even their veterinarian go through the adoption process. Luckily, I was approved! Willie is the ultimate family pet."

The Good Nurse

Espanola, New Mexico—For more than a week Ranger, a ten-year-old German shepherd, cared for a stray female mutt who had been trapped in a coyote snare underneath an abandoned camper. His incessant howling finally alerted a neighbor, who watched as Ranger came out from beneath the camper, got a mouthful of snow and then returned to his charge. When the neighbor offered Ranger a cup of canned tuna, he scooped up the cup and took it to the injured dog. As the incident was pieced together, the story spread throughout the Espanola area and more than thirty-five families offered to adopt the female stray, whose leg had to be amputated. As for Ranger, he returned home to proud owner Leo Martinez.

1994 Ken-L Ration Dog Hero of the Year Runner-up

Rambo Runs Interference

Clifton, North Carolina—Rambo, a four-month-old Rottweiler puppy, leapt into action when a rabid fox made a beeline toward owner John Tew, and intercepted the mad beast. Although Rambo survived this nightmare encounter, he unfortunately had not had all his shots because his owner thought that a dog had to be at least six months old to be inoculated against rabies. The daring puppy faced destruction if Tew couldn't come up with the money to pay for his six-month quarantine. When the story broke on the national news, more than fifty people offered to help pay for the medical costs. The generous pledges more than took care of Rambo's medical expenses, and Tew set up a fund with the balance to help other animals in the same plight.

Snellville, Georgia—Homer Mannin, who lives in a nursing home, has a lot of love to give to this Labrador puppy. The pup was placed in the home by the Shellville Women's Club as part of Gwinnett Humane Society's Pat-a-Pet program.

Zefiro & Luna/Liaison (L); Toni Tucker

CHAPTER 6

The Defenders

Leo the Lionhearted

Hunt, Texas—Leo, a courageous standard poodle, was bitten six times while defending owner Lana Callahan's two children, eleven-year-old Sean and nine-year-old Erin. The two siblings were playing with Leo near the Guadeloupe River when they stumbled upon a five-and-a-half-foot diamondback rattlesnake. Without hesitation, Leo leapt between the children and the venomous snake. The rattler struck again and again, leaving Leo with six bites to the head.

Nearly an hour passed before a veterinarian could be located. "Leo's vital signs were extremely weak. His face was so swollen, I couldn't see his left eyeball," said Dr. William Hoegemeyer. "Even with the latest in antivenins, dogs injured this seriously seldom survive."

But Leo survived. While his size and weight worked in his favor, the veterinarian attributed Leo's extraordinary will to live as the major factor. "Leo is a wonderful watchdog," said Mrs. Callahan. "He has always looked out for the kids and me."

1984 Ken-L Ration Dog Hero of the Year

Bloodied, Battered, but Unbowed

Priest River, Idaho—The most important thing that this show dog did was not in the ring. The stout-hearted collie, ironically named Hero, saved his three-year-old master, Shawn Jolley, from being stomped to death by an enraged horse.

With Shawn by her side, Mrs. Jolley was pitching hay down to the horses coming in to the barn from the pasture when, unnoticed, he toddled off. Suddenly, she heard her child scream and looked down in horror to see the little fellow running across the floor with a crazed horse racing after him. Instinctively, Mrs. Jolley shouted for Hero.

As Shawn tried to slide beneath a tractor at the end of the barn, his pants caught on a piece of machinery, leaving him at the mercy of the raging animal. The horse lunged forward, rearing up to stamp the life out of the tot.

In a blaze of glory, Hero came sailing through the air and crashed into the chest of the angry beast. Before the lethal hooves could once again threaten the helpless child, Hero seized the animal by the nose and grimly hung on. The furious horse swung the dog wildly from side to side, finally smashing him against a tractor tire, where Hero sank in a heap.

But Hero was up in an instant, flying back at the horse, which gave Mrs. Jolley an opening to pull Shawn safely out from underneath the tractor. As the horse began to pound Hero viciously, Mrs. Jolley joined the fray, beating the horse with a stick. Unexpectedly, the horse bolted out the door with Hero in hot pursuit. When the horse finally disappeared over the hillside, Hero dropped to the ground, with blood pouring from his nose and mouth.

Hero was rushed to a veterinarian forty-five miles away. His forefeet were crushed, five teeth were knocked out and four ribs were broken. Amazingly, just six weeks later, Hero was back in the ring, earning three more points toward his championship.

1966 Ken-L Ration Dog Hero of the Year

Hollywood Heroism

Chris Moorhead

Woodbridge, Virginia—Just like in the movies, Mickey, a ten-month-old Rottweiler, dove through a screen door to thwart the apparent abduction of her owner. Seventeen-year-old Dee Rafe screamed for her dog as she was being dragged out of her yard. Wasting no time, the angry pup attacked the assailant, drawing blood as she repeatedly bit him on his arms and legs. The thug fought back, punching the dog in the face before fleeing. Mickey received a shiner but soon recovered and is back on his watch by the front door.

Secret Weapon

Morris, Alabama—Meatball, a beloved German shepherd owned by Mr. and Mrs. Robert Keith, is really a top cop. Mrs. Keith was home alone chatting with her mother on the telephone when she heard someone pick up the extension in the empty greenhouse behind their home. Instead of reaching for a gun, she unleashed her secret weapon: Meatball. The intrepid dog surprised the intruder and chased him to the getaway car where an accomplice was waiting. As the would-be burglar jumped into the front seat, Meatball locked his jaws around his leg and held on as the vehicle sped away. The courageous canine was dragged along the road, suffering cracked toenails, cut pads and a bruised side, until he finally let go. Although the thieves were never caught, word quickly spread that no one messes with Meatball.

1977 Ken-L Ration Dog Hero of the Year

Ochre Knows a Felon

Forrest Park, Illinois—Ochre, a two-and-a-half-year-old Labrador Seeing Eye dog, chased a robber out of the garden apartment of his mistress, Mary Jane Schmidt. Even though the dishwasher was on and the television was blaring, the dog heard strange noises in the bedroom.

With the jingle of jewelry, Ochre sprang into action. The thief jumped out the window with the loyal lab in hot pursuit. Most of Mary Jane's valuables were saved. "Ochre defended our hearth and home," said the grateful owner.

The Night Stalker

New York, New York—Eastsider Cheryl Spadaro and her three-and-a-half-year-old Akita, Tiberius, were just finishing their evening walk when "Ty" began pulling her toward a parked car. Thinking that he just wanted a sniff, she followed. Suddenly, he started to growl. At that moment she saw a man wearing a hood crouching between two cars. As the assailant menacingly rose from his crouch, Tiberius leapt up on one of the cars and began barking wildly, while Cheryl screamed, "If you don't go away, my dog will bite your head off." The man got the message. As he began to slink away, Ty dropped back to the pavement and stayed by his mistress's side, barking until the man was out of sight.

The next night the man reappeared and Cheryl realized to her horror that he might be a stalker. The ever-protective Ty wasn't taking any chances and stared him down. The man fled, never to return.

Grizzly Bear Defeats His Match

Denali, Alaska—Grizzly Bear, an extremely gentle 180-pound, twenty-month-old St. Bernard owned by Mr. and Mrs. David Gratias, battled and finally routed a real grizzly bear that was mauling his mistress.

Around noon one cold spring day, while her two-year-old daughter, Theresa, was sleeping, Mrs. Gratias heard a noise in the backyard cabin behind the main building of a lodge they own and operate in a remote part of Alaska. Leaving open the only door to the cabin, she grabbed Grizzly Bear and went out to investigate.

To her horror, she discovered a young grizzly bear cub in the backyard. Assuming that his mother must be near, she raced back toward the open cabin door. But as she rounded the corner of the house, she came face to face with the mother grizzly.

The huge bear raised itself up to its full eight-foot height and lunged at her. Desperate to get to the open door to protect her daughter, she tried to sidestep the bear, but slipped on the icy ground. In a flash, the grizzly was upon her, raking her cheek with one paw while it sank the claws of the other deep into her shoulder.

Suddenly, the bear staggered backward as Grizzly Bear crashed into the angry beast with every ounce of his 180 pounds. Roaring with rage, the bear rebounded to attack Mrs. Gratias, but the heroic dog, maneuvering smartly, slashed at the bear with his teeth and paws, while managing to keep himself between the furious animal and his helpless mistress.

Mrs. Gratias, overcome with terror and loss of blood, lapsed into unconsciousness. When she came to, Grizzly Bear was licking her face, trying to revive her. She raced to the open door, to find Theresa inside, sleeping soundly. The mother bear and her cub had vanished; Mrs. Gratias's wounds eventually healed; and miraculously, Grizzly Bear survived the battle unscathed.

1970 Ken-L Ration Dog Hero of the Year

Chip Vinai (L) & Dale Spartas/Liaison

Guardian
Angels

King Crowns Attacker

Dorchester, Massachusetts—Thomas Perkins, seventy-seven, and King, his nine-year-old German shepherd, were enjoying a quiet evening at home when an intruder burst into their second-floor apartment shouting, "Give it up, old man." Perkins headed for the closet while King lunged at the thief and, despite being shot four times, drove him from the apartment. King survived with only the loss of a toe while his grateful owner said, "I have no friend but him. He saved my life."

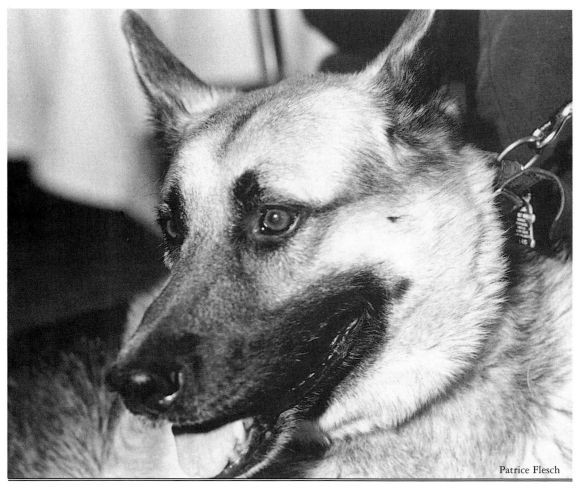

Patrice Flesch

Puppy Licks Sore Marriage

Sheffield, Massachusetts—When Mark and Sally Morris had an after-dinner marital tiff, Sally stormed out the front door for a walk in the snow. Their one-year-old Airedale, Rascal, accompanied her while Mark did the dishes. Getting ready for bed, he realized that Sally was taking an unusually long time to cool off. Suddenly, he heard her cry, "I'm really not OK." He found her clinging to the front door, barely able to move.

Sally had slipped and fallen on a patch of the ice, knocking herself out. For more than twenty minutes Rascal stayed by her side licking her face. When Sally finally awoke to a wet nose, the concerned puppy led her to the front door. The now-humbled husband carefully warmed his wife's face and hands to prevent frostbite. The next day the reconciled couple found the spot where Sally had fallen. The imprint of her face was etched in the ice.

Mixed Breed Does Thinking for Alzheimer's Victim

Mission Viejo, California—Buffy, a mixed breed, is a devoted companion to owner Don Kay, who suffers from Alzheimer's disease. Don's daughter, Merry, writes: "When Don can't quite remember just what it is he is going to say, Buffy is there. Buffy keeps him warm, never leaves him or becomes impatient, always understands him and only wants to be loved in return. And that is something Don can still do. Love. Buffy never tires, never strays, and never, never stops giving of himself to his owner. That's a hero."

    1993 Ken-L Ration Special Recognition Award

Doberman Averts Freak Drowning

Miles City, Montana—Sabbath, a Doberman pinscher owned by Mr. and Mrs. Don Neese, averted a freak drowning when two-and-a-half-year-old Buddy fell headfirst into a rain barrel. Mr. Neese had just returned from a motorcycle trip when he heard Sabbath barking furiously. Turning to look at the dog, he saw two tiny tennis sneakers protruding from the barrel. Mr. Neese yanked the child to safety, and Sabbath was hailed a hero.

    1982 Ken-L Ration Dog Hero of the Year Runner-up

The Canine Saint

Great St. Bernard's Pass—The tradition of mountain rescue dogs began nine hundred years ago by a monk who set up a hospice in a treacherous Alpine pass between Switzerland and Italy. The monk was canonized "St. Bernard" by the Church, and the dogs, whose daring avalanche rescues have become legendary, became known as St. Bernards.

The most fabled canine "Saint" was Barry, who saved dozens of trekkers in his lifetime. A statue in France honors one of Barry's best-known rescues, that of a small boy who was buried with his mother in an avalanche of snow. Although the boy's mother perished, Barry navigated the steep and icy mountain to get to the child, where he licked his face to revive him and then encouraged the boy to hang on while he pulled the youngster through the snow to safety.

A museum in Bern, Switzerland, has also memorialized Barry, who exists as a symbol not only for twenty-five hundred rescues in Great St. Bernard's Pass, but for all members of the gallant breed who continue to honor the tradition of heroism today.

Superdog Saves Superman

Kingston, New Jersey—Plushie, a motherly black Labrador, loved to look after the Ferrante family of seven children, ten cats, a horse and yet another dog. A favorite game of the children was to pretend to be so strong that they could push a car like Superman. Their mother found it amusing and let them play under her watchful eye as she was backing out of the garage. No one ever thought that the youngest child, three-year-old Philip, might get ideas of his own.

One day, when all his siblings were in school, Philip was alone in the driveway and decided to play Superman all by himself with a laundry truck. Unbeknownst to the driver, Philip got behind the truck and was holding onto the bumper ready to push. As the truck pulled out, Philip became frightened and hung onto the bumper with all his might. The truck picked up speed and began dragging the terrified child down the long driveway.

Philip's mother's sudden realization that her son was no longer in sight gave way to panic when the normally silent Plushie began barking insanely. Remembering the laundry truck, she ran screaming to the driveway to find her son hanging from the bumper and Plushie frantically running in front of the truck, barking and biting the tires.

The Lab's valiant efforts were rewarded when the puzzled driver stopped his truck and finally heard the chaos behind him. Philip's mother raced toward her son who was still clinging to the bumper with bloodied knees and shins, which were patched up with some disinfectant and lots of TLC. Plushie took center stage in the Ferrante family and was showered with thousands of hugs and kisses. Needless to say, the Superman game came to an end.

Benji, Come Home!

Lockport, New York—It's a good thing that three-year-old Benji Bodie brought his guardian angel along when he wandered away from home to "hunt tigers" one cool October afternoon. When he lost his way in a rural area dotted with farm ponds, Thumper, his St. Bernard pup, stayed by his side for twelve hours.

Benji's hunting expedition quickly turned into a nightmare for his parents, who frantically spread word about their missing son throughout the community. One thousand searchers covered acres of terrain, illuminating the chilly night with their lanterns and flashlights. At 2:00 A.M. rescuers heard Thumper barking in the distance and, following his cries, came upon Benji, curled up asleep at the still-barking dog's feet. Benji was covered with Thumper's hair, but was safe and sound beside the big, warm puppy.

In the morning, Benji's parents retraced the pair's steps. "They came within a few feet of a pond," says Mrs. Bodie, "but Thumper had the good sense to stay with Benji and keep him out of the water. You don't expect such devotion from a puppy. He's our sweetheart!"

1979 Ken-L Ration Dog Hero of the Year

Timing Is Everything

Euless, Texas—
Little Randy Saleh
went on his last
adventure fifteen
minutes before a
fence was to be
erected to corral the
wandering tot.
Fortunately, his St.
Bernard mix, Ringo,
tagged along.

Police fruitlessly
searched for the
child. Meanwhile,
motorist Harley Jones found himself stuck in traffic on the heavily traveled
Pipeline Road. After hearing a warning about a "mad dog in the road
ahead," Jones parked his car and went to investigate.

Rounding a curve he saw Ringo, resolutely stationed in the center of the
road, blocking traffic, leaping at the fender of any vehicle that dared move.
Cautiously approaching the frantic dog, he saw Randy playing happily in the
middle of the road.

Jones watched in wonder as the dog, after threatening a car, would rush
back to the child and nudge him to the side of the road. Apparently thinking it was some sort of game, the boy would immediately scurry back to the
center of the highway and sit there, laughing.

Jones talked soothingly to the protective animal, finally calming him
enough to pick up the child. With Ringo menacing him every step of the
way, Jones carried Randy to the side of the road. The dog then relaxed and
allowed the cars to pass.

1968 Ken-L Ration Dog Hero of the Year

Newfie Helps Boy to Speak

Shohola, Pennsylvania—Two Bears, a Newfoundland pup, was born with a disability that could eventually cripple her for life. But that's okay with her seven-year-old master Jason Nemac. This little boy with Down's syndrome suddenly stopped talking last May when the family's twelve-year-old Newfoundland mix passed away. When Two Bears arrived, Jason regained his speech. Their special bond grows stronger every day.

1993 Ken-L Ration Special Recognition Award

Athena Stops Traffic

Dunnellon, Florida—While walking his dog, Athena, teenager Brian Long, who suffers from diabetes, collapsed from insulin shock by the side of the road. After watching a long line of vehicles, including a school bus, pass by, the mixed breed planted herself in the middle of the road. Oblivious to the honks of angry motorists and her own safety, she refused to budge until a man finally stopped and discovered the prone teenager. The motorist called 911 and stayed with the boy and his dog until help arrived.

1994 Ken-L Ration Dog Hero of the Year Runner-up

Sheba, the Queen Bee

Nashville, Illinois—Sheba, an Alaskan Malamute, knocked down twenty-month-old Cassandra Vance and lay on top of her to protect her from a swarm of yellow jackets. Sheba received twenty-seven stings and nearly died, but Cassandra received just one!

1992 Ken-L Ration Dog Hero of the Year Runner-up

Heroic Dog Dies in Snake Attack

Lehigh Acres, Florida—When Klutz, a dachshund/beagle mix, saw his three-year-old mistress, Lindsey DeSanto, playing near a rattlesnake, he didn't think twice. He immediately attacked the five-foot rattler. While the battle ensued, Lindsey ran away unharmed. Klutz later died from snake bites.

  1992 Ken-L Ration Dog Hero of the Year Runner-up

Support Your Local Sheriff

Washington City, Utah—Two-and-a-half-year-old Lacy Merrifield was standing in her grandparents' front yard when a large, uninvited dog strayed onto the property and knocked her over. In an instant, Mo, her grandparents' full-blooded boxer, was at her side. Growling, shoving and baring his teeth, Mo ran the stranger off the range.

  1990 Ken-L Ration Dog Hero of the Year Runner-up

A Silent Cry Answered

Indian Valley, California—Boo, a two-year-old Newfoundland, pulled a drowning deaf-mute man from the rapids of the Yuba River. Boo had spotted Link Hill, unable to cry for help, struggling in the white water. The gentle giant dove in, grasped the man's wrist in his mouth and swam to shore, pulling him to safety.

  1995 Ken-L Ration Dog Hero of the Year Runner-up

Bailey Takes No Bull

Springfield, Missouri—Bailey, a three-year-old Chesapeake retriever/Labrador cross, fought off a 2,000 pound Belgian Blue bull to save the life of farmer Chester Jenkins. Jenkins had turned his back on the bull for only a second when the animal suddenly charged, crashed into him and tossed him several yards into a watering trough. The bull then pinned the man between the trough and the fence, raking his lethal hooves up and down Jenkins's back.

"I knew I was a dead man," said Jenkins. "Then I saw a blur of brown fur as Bailey charged at the bull." The dog went for the bull's head, bit his nose and ears and hung on tenaciously as the angry beast tried to throw him off. Fortunately, Bailey's ferocious attack gave the severely injured man time to squirm under the fence to safety.

Unharmed, the dog then ran for help. Finding the house empty, Bailey returned to help Jenkins get to the phone. When the paramedics arrived, the tireless dog met them in the yard to hurry them along.

Chester Jenkins was in the hospital for eleven days with crushed ribs, a broken shoulder, a punctured lung and internal bleeding. After a long recuperation, he is now fully recovered and back to farming. Said his son Dustin Jenkins, "Bailey saved my dad, just like Lassie."

1995 Ken-L Ration Dog Hero of the Year

Toni Tucker

Smarts

Collie Tugs Off Flaming Skirt

Niles, Ohio—One blustery March afternoon, Duke, the family collie, was playing in the backyard when his mistress, ten-year-old Penny Grantz, started a fire. The wind caused sparks to fly onto the girl's billowing skirt, which suddenly burst into flames. The panic-stricken girl raced toward the house twenty-five yards away.

Duke took in the situation at a glance. Barking loudly, he overtook the child and seized her flaming skirt in his jaws. Ripping and tearing, he pawed the skirt off her body, sustaining burns to his mouth.

Her father, a night worker who had been sleeping, heard the commotion and rushed Penny to the hospital. Her doctors said that without Duke's fearless action, Penny would have died.

1961 Ken-L Ration Dog Hero of the Year

There's Always Hope

Holcomb, Kansas—Hope's owners had a failure on their hands. Their pedigreed German shepherd was a bust as a show dog, and they had no idea just what, if anything, the dog could do, until one day she saved the life of their little boy.

While the family was unloading groceries, Gregory, their two-year-old son, slipped out of the apartment and wandered off. Fifty yards away, a train was rapidly approaching. Drawn by the flashing warning lights, the boy headed straight for the tracks.

A motorist leapt out of his car, yelling for the boy to stop, as he dashed toward the tracks. But the train roared in front of him, blocking the man's view. Fearing for the tot's life, he dropped to the pavement and searched for the boy beneath the passing train. Instead he saw Hope.

The intrepid dog had pushed the boy to the ground and then boldly positioned himself between Gregory and the thundering train. With one paw on the child at all times, Hope used her snout to nudge the boy backward out of danger until the train had safely passed.

Evidently unaware of his near-brush with death, Gregory's only comment was, "Choo-choo."

National German Shepherd Dog Club 1991 Hero Dog of the Year

Newfie Pup Saves Blizzard-bound Girl

Villas, New Jersey—During a severe blizzard, Villa, a black Newfoundland puppy owned by Linda Veit, rescued her neighbor, eleven-year-old Andrea Anderson. Sixty-mile-an-hour winds had driven the girl into a large snowdrift about forty feet from home. Disoriented, blinded by the blowing snow and unable to free herself, she screamed desperately for help.

Andrea's cries inspired the one-year-old puppy's first attempt at scaling the five-foot fence surrounding her run. Victorious, she bounded toward the girl eight feet away. Villa reassuringly licked the face of the panic-stricken child while circling her to clear the snow. Then the dog positioned herself so that Andrea could grasp her neck and be pulled out. The snow was so deep that Villa had to clear a path to lead the girl home. Andrea's mother, Bea Anderson, was shocked to see her shivering daughter clinging to the dog's neck.

According to her owner, Villa loves playing the hero. Exceptionally trainable, she is now adept at water rescues and loves to practice her craft on complete strangers.

1983 Ken-L Ration Dog Hero of the Year

Doberman Seizes Seizure

Muncie, Indiana—Tyler, a three-year-old Doberman pinscher, knew just what to do when eleven-year-old Jason Beard suffered an epileptic seizure in the middle of the night. The dog roused Jason's mother, Lela, from a deep sleep, grabbed her nightgown and dragged her into the boy's bedroom where she found him gasping for breath. Thanks to the quick-thinking Tyler, she was able to revive her son.

 1994 Ken-L Ration Dog Hero of the Year Runner-up

Tag Team Comforts Fallen Senior

Waurika, Oklahoma—Scout, a seven-year-old Labrador retriever, and Little Bit, an eleven-month-old Labrador mix, ganged up to help their eighty-four-year-old owner, Mary Gladys Baker, make it through the night. Worried that her dogs would get cold, Mrs. Baker went to get them an extra blanket. Wearing only in a nightgown and light coat, she slipped on the way to the doghouse and broke her hip.

 Concerned that his mistress was shivering, Scout dragged an old quilt from the doghouse to cover her while Little Bit squeezed through the storm door and retrieved Mrs. Baker's glasses. Both dogs then lay down beside their mistress to keep her warm until help arrived the next morning.

 1988 Ken-L Ration Dog Hero of the Year Runner-up

Sadie Saves the Day

Wisconsin—When Daniel Schnur was mending a fence over Labor Day weekend, he was ambushed by a charging bull. Sadie, his Brittany spaniel, leapt to the rescue, barking and biting at the angry bull's hooves. The scrappy canine picador distracted the bull, enabling Schnur to escape, and then scooted out of the impromptu ring, leaving behind the frustrated beast pointlessly pawing the earth.

 1994 Ken-L Ration Dog Hero of the Year Runner-up

Shepherd Outwits Snake

Nokomis, Florida—K.C., a German shepherd owned by Todd Hart, saved an employee of the family plumbing business from being bitten by a rattlesnake. K.C. was making her usual rounds with members of the crew when plumber Michael Nissley crawled under a mobile home and came face to face with an angry six-foot rattlesnake, coiled and ready to strike. K.C., who had dashed around to the back of the trailer, lunged and grabbed the snake from behind. Amazingly, both emerged unhurt.

    1982 Ken-L Ration Dog Hero of the Year Runner-up

The Long Journey Home

Canyon, Texas—While tending to his nine collies around midnight on a near-zero January night, Don Perkins stumbled in the darkness, badly injuring himself. Top dog Dee-Dog broke out of the kennel to assist his master while he tried to crawl the four hundred feet to his house. Instinctively, the collie took control, alternately lying next to Perkins's face to keep him warm, then barking to arouse and prod him forward. Although hospitalized with badly frostbitten feet, the man made a good recovery.

    1972 Ken-L Ration Dog Hero of the Year Runner-up

Don't Mess with Gus

Riverside, California—Taking out the trash one night, Steve Sage was surprised to find four intoxicated teenagers spoiling for a fight. Gus, his two-year-old Rottweiler, charged out the kitchen door, but instead of attacking, positioned himself directly in front of his master. Backing into his legs, the Rottweiler slowly pushed Sage six feet away from the delinquent youths. Only then did Gus advance to stare down the foursome, who, deciding not to take him on, fled.

    1995 Ken-L Ration Dog Hero of the Year Runner-up

Shepherd Saves Two Naughty Boys

Troy, Pennsylvania—Dutch, a fun loving German shepherd, dove into a frigid pond to rescue four-year-old Hugh Hawthorne and then barked for help to save the life of his three-year-old bother, Gordon.

Although the boys had been strictly forbidden by their parents to go near the pond without supervision, they "just forgot," romped out onto the dock and got into a scuffle. Suddenly, Gordon lost his balance and tumbled into the thirty-four degree water. Horrified, Hugh plunged in to save him. But neither child could swim a stroke.

Dutch took one look at the children thrashing about in the pond and leapt in after them. With powerful strokes, he swam to Hugh, grabbed his ankle in his jaws and paddled the sputtering boy to shore. Hearing Dutch continuously barking, their mother, who was nearly nine months pregnant, raced to the pond where she found Gordon floating face down. She, too, jumped in and towed her unconscious son to shore.

Although Gordon was blue in the face, she administered mouth to mouth resuscitation, and after several long minutes, she heard him gurgle. Although he apparently "died" three times, Gordon was finally revived at Troy Memorial Hospital and returned home the next day to hug his beloved dog.

1963 Ken-L Ration Dog Hero of the Year

Play Misty for Me

Massachusetts—When Chrissy, a fifteen-year-old husky/collie mix, dissappeared during a devastating blizzard, a human search party was dispatched but failed to find her. Dispirited, the search party decided to put Chrissy's best pal, Misty, a springer spaniel, on the case. In blinding snow she began digging frantically along a fence eventually exhuming Chrissy's left hind foot. Chrissy was rescued in the nick of time. Her leg had been trapped in the fence and, sadly, had to be amputated several weeks later. However, Chrissy continues to live a full life and the two canines are closer than ever.

1995 Massachusetts SPCA Gold Medal

Patrice Flesch

Shepherd Spares Woodsman

Martins Ferry, Ohio—Girl, a faithful three-and-a-half-year-old German shepherd, played a vital role in saving the life of her owner, Ray Ellis. Ellis had been cutting trees in the woods near his home when a sapling that had been pinned beneath a fallen tree suddenly sprang up, knocking him unconscious. The chainsaw slipped from his hand while it was still running, nearly severing his foot.

Girl stayed with him for a few minutes before running to the house to alert Ray's wife, Dorothy. "When I saw Girl coming, I thought Ray was on his way back, too," said Dorothy, "but she jumped up and down, then ran to the corner of the yard in Ray's direction and then ran back to me."

Girl led Dorothy to her stricken husband. After surgery and a series of casts on his ankle, Ray Ellis's foot finally healed. "Without Girl coming to get me," said Dorothy, "Ray surely would have bled to death."

1994 Ken-L Ration Dog Hero of the Year

Hairy Moments on the Colorado

Glenwood Springs, Colorado—Bo, a resourceful black Labrador retriever owned by Laurie and Rob Roberts, saved his mistress's life by pulling her from the Colorado River.

When an eight-foot rogue wave flipped their raft, Rob and Dutchess, their new puppy, were thrown clear, but Laurie and Bo were trapped underneath.

As the rapids carried Rob helplessly downstream, he frantically watched Bo emerge from beneath the raft, dive back underneath, and reappear towing Laurie by her hair. Free of the raft, Laurie grabbed Bo's tail and let the dog pull her across the current to shore. Thanks to the amazing Bo, the grateful family was happily reunited on the riverbank.

1982 Ken-L Ration Dog Hero of the Year

Don't Tangle with Tango!

Townsend, Washington—Luck was with Al Choate when he rescued ten-month-old Tango from the pound. A super dog from the get go, the thirteen-year-old border collie/Australian shepherd mix demonstrated outstanding bravery, loyalty and intelligence by risking her own life to save her master from an overly protective mother cow.

With Tango by his side, Mr. Choate went to check on two calves that had been born the night before when one of the mother cows unexpectedly became aggressive. The cow rammed into Choate's back, knocking him to the ground, and continued her assault, breaking his ribs and puncturing a lung. In jumped Tango. The dog lunged at the cow, gripped her jaw with her teeth, bit deeply and held on until her master crawled to safety.

Twelve years earlier Choate, who then raised livestock as a hobby, had been looking for a good shepherd dog and Tango's lineage seemed well-suited to his needs. He was right. Tango developed into a fine cattle dog, seemingly on her own.

"I remember, she used to follow me when I rounded up the cows for feeding," said Al Choate, while recovering from his injuries. "I'd walk down to the pasture and bring them up to the barn. One morning about four months after I got her, I went out, and by golly, there were all the cows waiting at the barn door. That pup had brought them up by herself. I didn't tell her to. She just did it on her own."

"I didn't know a lot about training a dog, but I didn't have to. Tango just knew what to do. Now, I can pick a cow out of the herd and tell Tango to go get it, and she'll bring it to me. There isn't any price tag you can put on her. She's just a wonderful dog."

1985 Ken-L Ration Dog Hero of the Year

Toni Tucker

CHAPTER 9

Thick and Thin

Herbert George Ponting

The Relay Race against Death

Nome, Alaska—The winners of this race across 650 miles of icy terrain were the children of Nome, Alaska, who were threatened by a deadly outbreak of diphtheria. Bad January weather had dashed any hope of an airborne delivery of the desperately needed serum. But a resourceful doctor in Anchorage had a brilliant idea: a sled dog relay to transport the serum from Nenana, the closest railroad stop, to Nome.

The race against death included twenty teams of Siberian huskies, malamutes and their mushers. The tag team pushed on through minus sixty degree temperatures, hazardous ice floes and blinding blizzards. Lead dog Togo, a Siberian husky, and musher Leonard Sepala braved the most treacherous leg of the journey. Finally, the vital serum was passed to Balto, a malamute, who with his musher Gunnar Kaasen blasted through the stormy weather to victory . . . for the children of Nome.

Left: Dog sled team at Castle Bay during the 1910-1913 South Polar Expedition.

Cocker Nips Disaster ... in the Hoof

Coeur d'Alene, Idaho—Taffy, a lovable cocker spaniel, saved her little master from a watery grave. Ken Wilson left his three-year-old son Stevie and Taffy in the yard where they couldn't get into trouble and, locking the gate behind him, went to a nearby corral to try out a saddle horse. However, a passing neighbor opened the gate, the child meandered out, and Taffy's rescue mission began.

The honey-colored cocker came bounding into the corral, startling Wilson. But the man did not pay much attention, believing that his boy was safe. Realizing that she was not getting through to Stevie's father, Taffy suddenly broke away and dashed toward the lake. A few minutes later, she reappeared dripping wet, barking at the top of her lungs and nipping at the horse's legs. Wilson was almost thrown from his mount.

With the sudden realization that the dog would never swim in the cold lake unless something was up, Wilson called out to his neighbor to see if his boy was still safe in the yard. When the neighbor replied that he had let the child out, Wilson jumped off his horse and raced after Taffy. At the edge of the lake, he saw Stevie's bright red parka floating on the surface.

Wilson lifted his unconscious son from the bottom of the clear four-foot-deep lake and administered mouth to mouth artificial respiration. For six hours, the youngster hovered between life and death. Just before midnight, Stevie's eyes flickered, and the first thing he saw was Taffy, standing vigil by his bed. An attending physician shook his head in wonderment at the pair.

1955 Ken-L Ration Dog Hero of the Year

Tough Love

Midland, Michigan—Jake, a 120-pound Rottweiler puppy, sank his teeth into the left thigh of two-and-a-half-year-old Jeffrey Charville, requiring nine stitches. But everybody thinks Jake's a hero. It's not that no one likes the little boy; they're delighted that he's still alive.

One afternoon, while Jake, Jeffrey and his mother were playing outside, Mrs. Charville scooted inside the house for a quick trip to the bathroom. Suddenly, Jake was barking. "My first instinct was, oh my God, the pond," recalled the boy's mother.

By the time she reached the pond, Jake had already pulled Jeffrey out of the water, dragged him onto the shore, and was licking his feet. An ambulance rushed the boy to the hospital. Jeffrey was fine except for the nine stitches he received to close the wound his beloved dog had given him during the rescue.

Later, both were given their just desserts: bones and grateful admiration for Jake; swimming lessons for Jeffrey.

Husky Hunts Snakes

Loveland, Colorado—Lady, a nine-year-old husky/retriever mix, bounded to the rescue when a group of children on a Labor Day outing disturbed a pack of rattlesnakes. "It sounded like a monster coming up from the ground," recalled Teresa Martines, "then I saw a snake. He didn't look very nice."

The dog attacked the snakes as the children ran for safety, but not before Teresa saw one of the snakes bite her pet. "The snake went up, came down, and then bit," she said. Lady continued battling the snakes until all the children were safe. She was bitten three times.

By the time Lady arrived at the veterinary hospital about fifteen miles away, her head had swollen and one eye was closed. Shaved and sore, Lady returned to her post guarding the Martines family with combat pay—hot dogs with her medicine.

Shepherd Puts Brakes on Rampaging Sow

Asheboro, North Carolina—Lady, a three-year-old German shepherd, rescued her owner, Burnic Wilson, from his angry, rampaging 600-pound sow. In trying to escape, Wilson had fallen and broken his arm. Fortunately, Lady arrived, leapt on the massive hog and bit her on the neck. The angry sow then directed her rage at Lady, who led the beast on a wild goose chase away from the injured farmer. "That old sow, she charged me. I tried to beat her off with a stick, but she just kept on coming." said Mr. Wilson. "I believe that sow would have torn me up. Lady is a wonderful dog."

Maiden Voyage

Newfoundland—The powerful Newfoundland's distinctive webbed feet were among the many characteristics that made the dog the breed of choice on the fishing circuit of the Grand Banks. So it comes as no surprise that Tang, a Newfoundland who lived on board the Ethie, performed one of the most daring maritime rescues of all time.

Back in 1919, the Ethie, with over ninety passengers on board, foundered on the rocky coast during a fierce winter gale. As the boat was hammered by the rising surf, the crew fired flares, drawing rescuers to the nearby beach. A mate volunteered to leap into the angry waters to swim a lifeline to the beach, but was lost forever in the surf.

With the ship in danger of breaking up, the captain turned to Tang and handed him the lifeline. With the rope in his teeth, the big dog cut through the frigid, churning sea, stormed the beach and delivered the line to the anxious crowd waiting on shore. The ship's crew rigged a makeshift harness and ferried the passengers, one by one, to shore until all were safe.

Kyle Danaceau/AP

Local Hero

Ocala, Florida—Three-year-old Blake Weaver's beloved Rottweiler, Samantha, saved his life by helping him survive for twenty hours in the Ocala National Forest.

When Blake wandered into the woods wearing only shorts and a T-shirt, he had Samantha, his guardian angel, by his side. As night fell and the temperature plunged, the dog nudged her charge beneath a bush and laid down on top of him to keep him warm. The next morning, Samantha led the traumatized child to a very relieved search party.

Samantha became a local hero. Talk show hosts courted her, Home Depot delivered a new doghouse and Sheriff Ken Ergle even deputized her as an honorary member of the emergency rescue squad.

Although Blake was initially plagued with nightmares, he now sleeps peacefully with Samantha by his side. Said Blake's mother, Dawn Weaver, "I love Rottweilers. I think they're beautiful animals."

That's Using Your Head!

Spokane, Washington—Goldie, a golden retriever owned by Barbara Thompson, saved her mistress's two-year-old grandson, Tommy Barnes, from certain drowning. Mrs. Thompson was walking in the backyard with her grandson and daughter, Cindy, when they suddenly noticed that Tommy was no longer right behind them. Fruitlessly searching the yard, they remembered the nearby pond, swollen from recent rains, and ran.

To their horror, the toddler was lying in the middle of the pond. Miraculously, Goldie was swimming by his side, using her nose to keep the boy face up. Each time the child rolled on his stomach, the dog turned him back over. Tommy was pulled from the pond unconscious and taken to the hospital where he spent several days recovering. Next to his bedside was a picture of Goldie, the conscientious canine who saved his life.

1982 Ken-L Ration Dog Hero of the Year Runner-up

Duke Dodges a Twister

Brookfield, Missouri—By barking at the darkening sky, Duke, a collie owned by Mr. and Mrs. William Fugate, warned them of a tornado that was barreling toward their farm. The couple, who had no storm cellar, jumped in their truck and sped away minutes before the twister devastated their property.

1975 Ken-L Ration Dog Hero of the Year Runner-up

The Dog Who Came in from the Cold

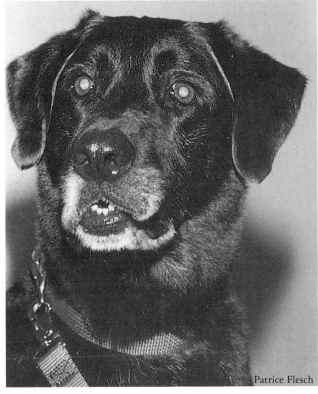
Patrice Flesch

Raynham, Massachusetts— Huddled beneath his black Laborador retriever, Shadow, Greg Holzworth refused to believe that he was going to freeze to death in the woods.

Following an afternoon of homework, the twelve-year-old boy and his dog set off for a frolic in the woods. Eventually, they found themselves in an unfamiliar swamp. Eight inches of fresh snow had covered their tracks. They knew that they were lost.

"I was scared and I was wicked cold, but I wasn't thinking about panicking. I was thinking about staying warm and getting home," said the freckle-faced youngster. "I just lay there and Shadow lay next to me and then he got up on top of me. My dog kept me warm."

For nine hours more than one hundred police officers, firefighters, family members and volunteers searched for the boy and his dog. When Greg finally heard the rescue party calling his name, his throat was too raw from the cold to answer. Shadow barked instead.

Greg and Shadow were found cold and wet but still alive. "I was there and I can't even imagine that kid being outside in that cold that long," said volunteer Francis Leary, "I hate to think about what would have happened without that dog."

Dalmatian Puts Fallen Rider Back in Saddle

Harry Heleotis

Hyde Park, New York—Tuser, an eight-year-old Dalmatian, likes nothing better than to tag along when his mistress Laura Bachko goes riding on her bay gelding, Flying Colors. However, while taking a New Year's Day shortcut, Colors slipped and went down, rolling on top of Laura. Slashed from shoulder to hip, the riderless Colors struggled to get up and ran for the barn.

Laura was not so lucky. A rock had wedged between her head and her helmet, crushing part of her skull. Unconscious, she lay in the woods. But loyal Tuser stayed with Laura and licked and nudged her until she regained consciousness. Dazed and confused, but finally able to stand, Laura put her faith in Tuser, who led her back to the barn.

At the hospital, Laura suddenly became comatose with fixed and dilated pupils—the medical definition of death. After five hours of emergency surgery, she regained consciousness and began asking about her horse and beloved dog.

Six months later, with Tuser trotting beside her, Laura was back in the saddle again, but wearing a new riding cap. Her old helmet, still covered with Tuser's fur where he licked her wound, sits proudly on Laura's bedside table.

Golden Retriever Helps Boy Skip Icy Bath

Evansville, Indiana— Merle, a sixty-five-pound, two-year-old golden retriever, fell through the ice while chasing a stick. Terrified his dog was in trouble, ten-year-old Glenn "Sam" Henderson tried to save her, but fell in as well. A neighbor heard the boy's cries for help and called the Perry Township Volunteer Fire Department.

Witnesses credit Merle with saving Sam's life. "We've never had anything quite like this. The whole time it looked like the dog was behind him, nudging him, keeping him up and pushing him toward the ice," said Goeff L. Rupe, medical officer for the fire department. "Once we got Sam into the boat, the only thing he said was, 'Get my dog.'"

Unhurt in the icy plunge, Merle swam to shore, and waited on the bank while Sam was rowed to safety. She continued pacing nervously outside the ambulance while Sam was stripped, dried off, and wrapped in a blanket. The youngster was rushed to Deaconess Hospital and treated for hypothermia.

The pair were reunited at home. "We'll have to find a nice steak bone for Merle," said the boy's father. As for Sam, Mr. Henderson said, "He can have whatever he wants to eat today but, much to his dislike, he's got some homework to do."

John Duricka/AP

Leader of the Pack

Nome, Alaska—Only extraordinary dogs are strong enough to endure the challenges of the trans-Alaska Sled Dog Race known as the Iditarod. And only the most courageous dogs are chosen to lead their eighteen-member packs over more than a thousand grueling miles of winter weather. Granite was such a dog. Leader of four winning teams, this Alaskan husky has demonstrated an uncanny ability to anticipate danger and uncommon bravery.

While racing across the ice, Granite sensed that the footing had changed and that the ice was about to give way. He picked up speed and reached the beach just as the sled crashed through the ice. The valiant dog struggled forward through the slush, finally pulling the sled and his mistress, Susan Butcher, to safety.

When the team was viciously attacked by an angry cow moose, most of the dogs recoiled as if they were "trying to melt into the snow," Butcher recalled. But not Granite, who stood his ground and defended his team. Eventually the moose got past him and began mauling the rear dogs. Granite didn't let up. He attacked the moose from behind, relentlessly, until a wild kick to his head flattened him against a tree.

As the moose's assault turned deadly, killing two of the dogs and injuring eleven others, a competitor arrived and shot the crazed animal. Butcher's team was out of the race, but Granite survived. He had shown that special something that separates the leader from the pack. Together, Granite and Susan Butcher went on to lead their team to victory again . . . and again . . . and again.

National Air & Space Museum

Laguna Photo/Liaison

Toni Tucker

VOICE OF BRITAIN

CHURCH

UPI/Corbis-Bettmann

CHAPTER 10

My Best Friend

Toni Tucker

Two for the Price of One

Los Angeles, California—In a heroic double-header, Top, a child-loving Great Dane owned by Axel Patzwaldt, saved two youngsters from certain death.

The huge dog's exploits began one spring morning when a lucky eleven-year-old girl was allowed to take him out for a walk. Crossing the street, she failed to notice that a large truck was barreling down the road. Top, barking loudly, jumped in front of the girl and pushed her backward out of the way. The girl was unhurt, but Top was broadsided by the truck, his right rear leg shattered.

The gallant Dane was rushed to the hospital and his leg was placed in a cast. For seven weeks, he limped about painfully. But one week after his cast was removed, Top was at it again, saving the life of a drowning boy.

With Top's cast off, Patzwaldt let him out of the apartment to play by the swimming pool. Seconds later, Top came bounding to the door, soaking wet and barking at the top of his lungs. His master and other residents ran after the wildly barking Great Dane to find two-year-old Christopher Conley at the bottom of the six-foot-deep pool.

Patzwaldt, a former lifeguard, dove into the pool and brought the lifeless child to the surface. He began mouth-to-mouth resuscitation and managed to arouse a spark of life. Paramedics arrived and eight hours later, emergency room doctors pronounced Christopher out of danger.

1969 Ken-L Ration Dog Hero of the Year

Collie Halts Slide

Jim Thorpe, Pennsylvania—Laddie displayed Lassie-like good sense when he saved his master, twelve-year-old Ron Gerenser, from falling off a treacherous rocky ledge. With Laddie on the leash, the two buddies were hiking along the top of a mountain ridge when Ron slipped and tumbled down a thirty-five-foot embankment.

The boy was still holding the leash when he finally came to a stop. Fortunately, Laddie had landed several feet above Ron and had planted his feet firmly into the snow to prevent the two of them from falling further down the mountain.

Ron was in deep trouble, lying just inches away from a ledge that dropped 140 feet straight down. When he tried to inch his way back up the mountain, Laddie barked and blocked his path. Instinctively, the collie sensed that any attempt to move might cause a fatal fall.

Ron began calling out for help. After an endless hour, the pair were spotted from the town below. Rescuers used aerial ladders and ropes to scale the cliff. Thanks to Laddie, the two pals were unharmed.

1982 Ken-L Ration Dog Hero of the Year Runner-up

No Beach Day for Gidget

Warren, Ohio—Gidget, a poodle owned by Dr. and Mrs. Howard Krause, saved two lives when she ignored house rules by climbing the stairs to the second floor in order to alert a young boy that a fire was burning on the first floor. Once aware of the danger, the boy carried his ninety-one-year-old grandmother to safety.

1975 Ken-L Ration Dog Hero Of The Year Runner-up

Little Dog, Big Courage

Johnson City, Tennessee—When a vicious chow leapt over a fence and attacked two sisters, Brandy, their lovable cocker spaniel, jumped in to defend them. The gallant little dog courageously placed himself in front of his charges, refusing to retreat until a neighbor arrived and began beating the chow with a broom. The chow finally relented, but not before he had bitten fourteen-year-old Jamie Kissel. "He locked his jaw on my leg and wouldn't let go," she said. Her sister, four-year-old Danielle, was unharmed, but Brandy was not so lucky. He was bitten on his front legs, shoulder and neck. "Brandy is only about half the size of the chow. He really got chewed up," said Joy Kissel, the girls' mother. "He's lucky he's alive. He really stood his ground."

This Dalmatian Is Not Decoration

Newport, South Carolina—Spuds, a spunky Dalmatian, upheld the honor of his breed by saving his fifteen-year-old master Dirk Tanis and housemate, Gizmo, a five-month-old kitten, from a quick-moving kitchen fire. After preparing a meal, Dirk had fallen asleep. He was awakened by his dog chewing his hand. To his shock, flames had reached the kitchen ceiling, the microwave was melting down and smoke was everywhere.

Tanis sprinted from the house to call 911 while Spuds grabbed Gizmo by the scruff of the neck and hauled her outside. Dirk's mother was amazed. "We always talk about how dumb Spuds is. We didn't think he would have the presence of mind to do something like that."

Even fire captain Ben Roach was impressed. "If I had a pet, I'd like to have a dog just like Spuds," said Roach, surveying the blackened kitchen. "You always see Lassie on TV doing neat things. Well, this dog did a real neat thing."

1991 William O. Stillman Award

St. Bernard Unties Cement Shoes

Anchorage, Alaska—The amazing exploit of Mijo, a 180-pound St. Bernard, began with an after-dinner walk and ended in the lifesaving rescue of his thirteen-year-old mistress, Philiciann Bennett.

Freed of her leash but wearing a neck chain, Mijo was romping at the edge of a water-filled gravel pit with Philiciann and her eleven-year-old brother, Mitchell, when the rain-softened ground suddenly slid beneath the girl. Philiciann tried to "push off" but, to her horror, sank deeper and deeper. Unable to free her feet and with the water up to her chin, the panic-stricken girl screamed for help.

Mitchell began scrambling down the steep embankment to help his hopelessly mired sister, but Mijo had already come to the rescue. After circling in front of the girl, the dog dove down and came up directly in front of her. Philiciann made a desperate grab for the dog's chain and hung on.

With the first of her powerful strokes, the huge St. Bernard yanked her feet free and headed for open water. Towing the almost dead weight of the 105-pound teenager, Mijo swam to a nearby bank and pulled Philiciann to safety. Watching in amazement, Mitchell carefully made his way along the bank to comfort his sister and hug their dog.

1967 Ken-L Ration Dog Hero of the Year

Follow the Leader

Washington, Connecticut—An unseasonably warm, early spring day inspired Emma Sweeney and Jed, her yellow Labrador retriever, to go hiking in the Steep Rock Nature Preserve. Although the paths were wet and mucky with the melting snow, the pair so enjoyed their adventure that before long they had meandered away from their customary route. As they turned around for the trek home, Emma realized that she had no idea where she was.

With the sun going down, she nervously tried several paths, but failed to find any familiar trails. Hopelessly lost, frustrated and scared, she sat down and began to panic. Jed, who had the boundless energy of a young Lab, started barking. Emma was sure he just wanted to play until it finally dawned on her that Jed was trying to tell her something.

Placing her hopes in her young dog she shouted, "Jed, let's go home!" Immediately, the dog began to head in an unlikely direction, his nose to the ground sniffing for clues. He picked his way carefully through pines, hemlocks, fallen trees and mud for at least an hour. Emma was worried that the dog's usual keen sense of smell would fail him, but Jed knew where he was going. His blond coat shown in the moonlight as they reached the entrance to the preserve, where a relieved search party that included her boyfriend and the police had gathered.

From that day forward, it was Jed who took Emma for walks in Steep Rock, not the other way around.

Pashka's Birthday Present

Bassford Canyon, California—An airplane ride to a birthday lunch seemed like a good present for Steve Bennett's twenty-second birthday. For fun, his roommate, pilot Leo Piggott, also invited Pashka, Steve's four-month-old Afghan pup, to tag along.

Lunch was terrific, but dessert was a disaster. The single engine plane ran into a storm in remote Bassford Canyon. When the visibility dropped to zero, the Piper plowed into the canyon, ripping the plane from wing to wing. The cockpit continued on, roaring up the hillside, finally crashing and ejecting the two men.

Steve was immobilized with a broken pelvis, Leo suffered a dislocated shoulder and the puppy was nowhere to be found. Leo struggled in the rain in search of help. As night fell, he worried about his friend, freezing in the rain, and wondered about the missing dog. Fortunately, Pashka had made his way back to his injured master.

Nearly a day later, Leo reached the home of Charles and Mattie Lou Jeffries, who first thought the disheveled man was an escaped convict. When he collapsed recounting his story, however, they summoned help.

Several airborne rescue missions failed because of the weather, but finally a three-man team in a jeep discovered Bennett and his faithful companion curled up amidst the wreckage. As the rescue workers lifted the injured man onto a stretcher, Pashka tried to leap on board.

Bennett survived his birthday ordeal thanks to Pashka, who gave him the will to live through that awful night. "I prayed and I hoped, but I never gave up," recalled Steve Bennett, "Pashka was my warm and friendly comforter."

1967 William O. Stillman Award

Wily Willy Thwarts Faulty Furnace

Los Alamos, New Mexico—Willy the weimaraner awakened his owner, Betty Souder, moments before they both succumbed to carbon monoxide poisoning from a leaky furnace. The nine-year-old dog pawed and pawed his mistress until she stirred from a hazy sleep. When Ms. Souder finally stood, she knew something was wrong. "I felt so dizzy and awful," she said, "I thought I must be having a stroke." When she saw that Willy was also weaving, she realized that they were both in serious trouble. Mrs. Souder tried to call for help, but kept dropping the phone. On her third attempt, she reached a friend. According to her doctor, if Willy had let his owner sleep just a few minutes longer, she would never have made the call.

1992 Ken-L Ration Dog Hero of the Year

CynthiaMatthews

Beth S. St. George

CHAPTER 11

Guts

Tass

First Hero in Outer Space

Moscow—Intelligent, tough and fearless, Laika had all the qualities of a great astronaut. But Laika was a dog.

In October of 1957, the Soviet Union scored a stunning victory in the space race with the United States by launching Sputnik I, which orbited the earth for weeks. In a dramatic encore, the Russians launched Sputnik II, this time with a passenger on board—eleven-pound Laika.

The world watched as the weightless Laika circled the globe. Strapped in a harness, she was able to move about the cabin for short periods while earth-bound scientists monitored her heartbeat and respiration. Her vital signs returned to near normal in orbit after a threefold increase during the launch, demonstrating that human beings could survive in space.

However, the Russians had overlooked just one thing: how to get Laika safely back to earth. Her oxygen supply ran out after six days and Laika died in space. Five months later, Sputnik II entered the earth's atmosphere and burned.

Three years later, the Russians sent two more dogs into space, Belka and Strelka, who thankfully returned safely to earth. When Strelka later gave birth, Soviet Premier Nikita Khrushchev gave one of the postorbital pups to President John F. Kennedy.

Surprise Attack Stuns Gunmen

Houston, Texas—Chelsea, a brave golden retriever, risked her life to save her master, Chris Dittmar, and a neighbor from two armed assailants. The men were chatting in the driveway with Chelsea at their feet when two strangers approached and asked the time. Seconds later, the two friends were staring down the barrels of a pair of loaded revolvers.

Terrified, neither man could utter a word. Suddenly, a deep-throated growl cut through the night air as Chelsea leapt toward the gunmen, her body outstretched and her mouth opened wide. Dittmar was almost as shocked as the startled gunmen. "Because it was dark, all you could see was her white teeth."

Panicked, one of the assailants fired twice hitting Chelsea in the shoulder. Dittmar and his friend ran for cover while the second assailant aimed and fired. Bullets whizzed by as they bolted for the garage.

After the police arrived, Dittmar began a frantic search for Chelsea. Two blocks from home, she limped out from some bushes. "It was the happiest moment of my life," Dittmar said.

The fearless dog was rushed to an all-night animal clinic where she underwent surgery to remove the bullet. Chelsea was off her feet for three months, noise-shy for six, but is now fully recovered. She doesn't even walk with a limp.

1990 Ken-L Ration Dog Hero of the Year

The Christmas Dog Who Kept on Giving

Granite Falls, Washington—When a fire broke out in their utility room the day after Christmas, King, Mr. and Mrs. Howard Carlson's German shepherd mix, was asleep in the family room. Instead of making a speedy exit through the sliding glass doors that had been left open for him, King fought his way into the fire, clawing and chewing until he broke through the hot utility room door.

The dog charged through the burning room into the bedroom where sixteen-year-old Pearl Carlson was sleeping. Whining, he nudged her until she awoke. Then the pair rushed to the parent's bedroom. Mr. Carlson, who had a lung condition, could not move as quickly as his wife and daughter, but King remained at his side until he was safely outside.

Although fire consumed their house, the Carlsons were safe. However, King was badly burned on his paws, had a gash on his back and splinters in his mouth. Under the careful watch of the Carlsons, he has made a full recovery. "When King joined our family on Christmas Eve five years ago," said Mrs. Carlson, "we never dreamed that he would someday save our lives."

1981 Ken-L Ration Dog Hero of the Year

Guard Dog Defends Post

Newark, New Jersey—Mombo, a German shepherd mix trained by the renowned Captain Haggerty, boldly defended his turf when an auto parts storage yard was raided by a band of thieves. Alerted by the ensuing chaos, the security guard arrived to find at least six terrified banditos hightailing it through the tall grass.

As the guard bathed the bruised and bleeding Mombo, he found what appeared to be a large hunk of caked blood on his hindquarters. Upon closer inspection, he learned that the fearless four-footed soldier had driven off the attackers in spite of the fact that an arrow, broken off at the shaft, was painfully buried in his thigh.

This Bud's for You

John's Island, South Carolina— Fortunately, a fearless fourteen-month-old St. Bernard named Budweiser was a member of the Carter family when an explosion sent flames rocketing through their home.

While Mrs. Carter rounded up four of her six grand-children, Budweiser charged into the house, grabbed the youngest by her shirt and pulled her to safety. He raced back into the blazing building, and returned victorious, dragging the last child by her arm. As he tried to enter a third time to rescue the family Chihuahua, he was driven back by intense flames. Soon after, the roof collapsed and the house was reduced to cinders.

1973 Ken-L Ration Dog Hero of the Year Runner-up

Pit Bull Braves Roaring River

Imperial Beach, California—Heavy rains caused a dam to break several miles upstream on the normally sedate, three-foot-wide Tijuana River, unleashing a roaring, deadly torrent. For thirty days the nonstop heroism of Weela, a courageous sixty-five-pound American pit bull terrier, saved thirty people, twenty-nine dogs, thirteen horses and one cat, all of whom might otherwise have perished.

Weela's rescue efforts began when her owners, Lori and Daniel Watkins, recognized her extraordinary ability to sense quicksand, dangerous dropoffs and mud bogs. The threesome worked for six hours battling heavy rains, strong currents and floating debris to reach a friend's ranch and rescue twelve dogs. In another instance, Weela led a rescue team to thirteen horses that had been stranded on a large manure pile completely surrounded by flood waters. Thankfully the team was able to bring the horses to safe ground.

Over the next month, Weela braved the perilous river wearing a harnessed backpack filled with thirty pounds of dog food to feed seventeen dogs and a cat who were stranded on an island. On one of many return trips, Weela came upon a group of thirty people who were about to cross where the water ran fast and deep. By barking and running back and forth, Weela led the group upstream to shallower, slower water where they could safely make it across.

Reflecting upon the devastating flood, Lori Watkins said, "Weela was constantly willing to put herself in dangerous situations. She always took the lead except to circle back if someone needed help."

Winner 1993 Ken-L Ration Dog Hero of the Year

Shepherd Routs Rabid Raccoon

Patrice Flesch

Weymouth, Massachusetts – Kelsey, a two-year-old German shepherd, saved her eight-year-old mistress from the jaws of a rabid raccoon.

Little Ashley Gillen had been playing in the woods about thirty yards from home when a thirty-pound raccoon suddenly charged her. Within seconds the coon was biting and scratching the girl. Her alarmed mother, Judy Gillen, ran from the house to find her screaming daughter frantically trying to scale a four-foot-high fence.

Kelsey bounded out of the front gate in hot pursuit to attack the vicious beast. Ashley fled while the shepherd cornered the raccoon beneath a parked car and prevented its escape until police arrived.

Tests revealed that the raccoon was rabid, and the painful, life-saving rabies serum had to be administered to all hands, including Kelsey. A relieved and grateful Judy Gillen said, "If it weren't for Kelsey, my daughter would have been severely mauled by that raccoon."

1994 Massachusetts SPCA Gold Medal

Dangerous Dive

Cleveland, Ohio—In a daring rescue in the Metroparks Rocky River Reservation, Woodie, a collie mix owned by Rae Anne Knitter, dove off an eighty-foot cliff to come to the aid of his mistress's fiancé, Ray Thomas. Ray had lugged his camera equipment up the hill to capture the view while Rae Anne and Woodie waited patiently on the path. At the peak he suddenly disappeared.

Woodie immediately began dragging Rae Anne up the hill. Convinced that something was wrong, she unleashed the dog and followed her. At the summit, Rae Anne looked in horror at the eighty-foot drop. Thomas lay motionless face down in a stream with Woodie by his side.

Sensing her friend's need, Woodie had jumped after him, breaking both hips in the fall. Despite her injuries, the valiant dog struggled to nudge Ray's face out of the water to keep him from drowning until rescue workers arrived.

Ray spent two months in the hospital undergoing treatment for multiple fractures in his back and arm. In addition to internal injuries and broken bones, Woodie underwent a personality change. "She's more affectionate than ever," said Rae Anne, "as if she realizes how lucky they are to be alive."

1980 Ken-L Ration Dog Hero of the Year

Blaze of Glory

Timewell, Illinois—Blaze, a beautiful white-faced collie, saved two-and-a-half-year-old Dawn Hecox from the ravages of an angry sow. Little Dawn was playing in the yard of the family farm when she decided to crawl through a fence to get a better look at some baby pigs. The infuriated mother sow charged, knocked Dawn to the ground and began mauling the child.

Despite his ever-present fear of the massive hog, Blaze cleared the fence with a single bound and attacked the sow so savagely that she backed off, leaving time enough for Dawn to escape through the fence.

Her stunned parents rushed the shocked and bleeding child to the hospital. With four teeth knocked out and numerous bites, the child was in critical condition for two days and under the constant care of physicians for two weeks before recovering.

The birth of Blaze had been a surprise. While the Hecox family was dogsitting for Blaze's mother, she unexpectedly gave birth. As a reward for taking care of the mother and pups, the owner gave them Blaze, the biggest, handsomest and most courageous of the litter.

1957 Ken-L Ration Dog Hero of the Year

Chips Goes to War

Sicily, Italy—Chips, a German shepherd/collie/husky mix, was one the first of four dogs of the Army's K-9 Corps to cross the Atlantic during World War II and the only one to be awarded the Silver Star and the Purple Heart.

Chips and the rest of the Seventh Army, under the command of General George Patton, assembled off the coast of Sicily. Before dawn on July 10, 1943, they boarded amphibious crafts and attacked. In the lead landing craft, Chips and the other soldiers encountered heavy fire from the entrenched Italian gun positions.

Chips and his unit were pinned down on the beach. Although a number of soldiers tried to restrain Chips, he singlehandedly stormed an Italian bunker. Even after suffering scalp and hip wounds, Chips continued his charge.

The next thing the members of Chips's unit saw were Italians running from the bunker screaming. Then Chips emerged, dragging an enemy soldier by the neck. Finally, the three remaining Axis soldiers ran from the bunker and surrendered.

Chips was taken to a field hospital for treatment of his wounds. Besides the scalp and hip wound, Chips's mouth was seriously burned. Evidently, he injured his mouth when he grabbed a hot machine gun from an enemy soldier.

Chips received his Silver Star and the Purple Heart from General Lucian Truscott Jr. calmly. However, some months later, when he was congratulated by Supreme Allied Commander Dwight D. Eisenhower, he bit the general on the hand.

The Ken-L Ration Dog Hero Program

Although every dog is a hero to its owner in one way or another, there are hundreds of dogs in America who have performed truly brave feats in the face of danger. In 1954 Ken-L Ration decided to recognize these outstanding achievements of our canine companions and began the Dog Hero Awards.

Over the past forty-two years, Ken-L Ration Dog Heroes have saved the lives of more than eighty children and adults.

Dog Heroes come in all shapes and sizes. The largest were the St. Bernards Mijo (1967) and Grizzly Bear (1970), who both weighed in at 180 pounds. The smallest Dog Hero was Mimi (1972), a miniature poodle who stood only twelve inches high.

Dog Heroes include twelve mixed breeds, five German shepherds, five St. Bernards, five collies, two poodles, one cocker spaniel, one Shetland sheepdog, one Great Dane, one Chesapeake Bay retriever, two Labrador retrievers, one Weimaraner and one American pit bull terrier. Males outnumber females twenty-five to seventeen.

Geographically, California heads the list with eight Dog Heroes. Four have lived in Texas; three in New Jersey and Washington; two in Alaska, Florida, Idaho, Montana, North Dakota and Ohio; and one each in Alabama, Colorado, Connecticut, Illinois, Massachusetts, Minnesota, Missouri, New Mexico, New York, Pennsylvania, South Carolina and Tennessee.

Acknowledgments

The authors wish to express their gratitude to Doris Straus for yet another inspired design; to Christine Schillig for acquiring this project and bringing it to fruition; to Stephanie Bennett for her undeviating support; to Jim Buck, Jim Buck Dogs; to Richard Abbott, Stephen Kuusisto, and Eileen Scully, Guiding Eyes For The Blind; to Ken-L Ration for establishing the Dog Hero program; to Michel Bernard, Susan Carolonza, John Clark, Jean Yves Mallet and Valerie Zars, Liaison International; to Melissa Bassett and Paul Capozzoli, Massachusetts Society for the Prevention of Cruelty to Animals; to Jessie Vicha, McDowell & Piasecki Food Communications; to Marilyn Mode, New York City Police Department; to Assistant Chief Fire Marshal Louis Garcia, Michael Regan and Robert Leonard, New York City Fire Department; to Helen Cannavale for her diligent picture research; to Mary Dearborn who made the complicated simple; to Katharine Marx for her finishing touches; to Lisa Newlin who organized everything; to Christine Shaw who kept the hard drive spinning; and to our friend and colleague Roger Straus III for pinch hitting when the chips were down.